Iñuksuk

Northern Koyukon, Gwich'in & Lower Tanana

1800–1901

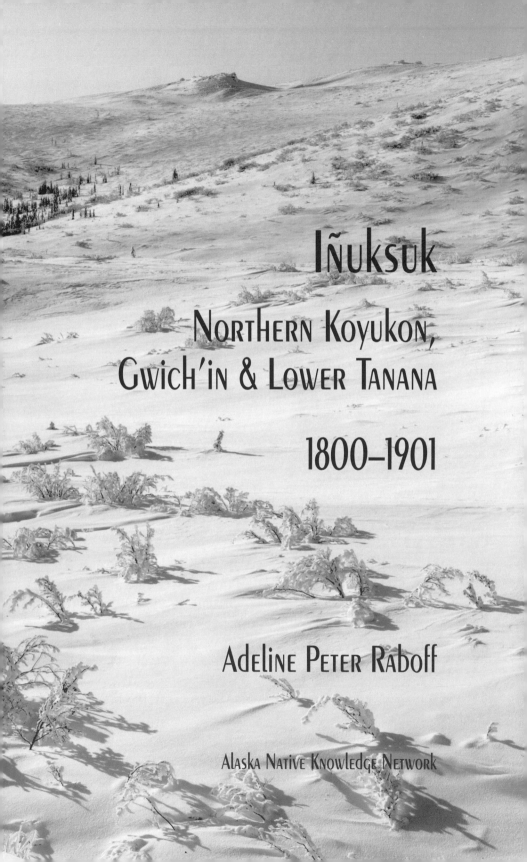

Iñuksuk

Northern Koyukon, Gwich'in & Lower Tanana

1800–1901

Adeline Peter Raboff

Alaska Native Knowledge Network

Alaska Native Knowledge Network, Fairbanks AK 99775-6730
© 2001 by Adeline Peter Raboff
All rights reserved. Published 2001
Printed in the United States of America

Elmer E. Rasmuson Library Cataloging in Publication Data:

Raboff, Adeline Peter.
 Inuksuk : northern Koyukon, Gwich'in & lower Tanana, 1800–1901 /
 by Adeline Peter Raboff.—Fairbanks : Alaska Native Knowledge
 Network, 2001.
 p. : ill., maps ; cm.
 Includes bibliographical references.
 ISBN 1-877962-37-6
 1. Koyukon Indians—History—19th century. 2. Gwich'in Indians–
 History—19th century. 3. Tanana Indians—History—19th century. 4.
 Athapascan Indians—History—19th century
 I. Title.

 E99.A86 R33 2001

Title page photograph: Early snowfall, east of Kurupa Lake, © Dennis Witmer

This book is the result of a wish expressed by my father, the late Steven Tsee Gho', Tsyaa Tsal Peter, Sr. and dedicated to Ernest "Tiger" S. Burch, Jr., whose work is a true gift.

Stephen Steven Tsee Gho' Tsyaa
Tsal Peter, Sr. Photograph taken in
Fort Yukon, Alaska c. 1925.
Courtesy of the Raboff Collection.

Contents

List of Figures

List of Figures, con't.

Introduction

The history of the Saakił Hʉt'aane Koyukon, Nendaaghe Hʉt'aane Koyukon, and Too Loghe Hʉt'aane Koyukon and the Too Tleekk'e Hʉt'aane, Di'hąįį Gwich'in, and Taghe Chox Xut'ana Lower Tanana is a history of the upper Kobuk, Noatak, Colville, John, and Koyukuk rivers and the Yukon River from the confluence of the Tozitna River and Lower Birch Creek. It concerns five nations which no longer exist as separate groups. However, their descendants continue to live along the upper Koyukuk River valley and along the Yukon River. None of the groups have been extensively documented or studied individually because so little was known about them.

Thankfully, there have been hints about them in the writings of Lieut. L. A. Zagoskin, a Russian Explorer (1842); Alexander Hunter Murray and William Lucas Hardisty of the Hudson's Bay Company (1847–51); Rochfort Maguire and Doctor John Simpson of the British naval ship *HMS Plover* (1854); Robert Kennicott (1862); and Archdeacon Robert McDonald and W. W. Kirkby of the Anglican Church (1862–80) during the initial contact period. Often times there is little more than a sentence or paragraph about these groups in those accounts.

After 1866, there are the accounts of American explorers, military personnel, traders, and missionaries: Frederick Whymper (1867), Francois Xavier Merçier (1868), Captain Charles W. Raymond (1869), W. H. Dall (1870), George M. Stoney (1885), Jules L. Prevost of the Episcopal Church (1892), F. C. Schrader

(1899), Lieut. John C. Cantwell of the Steamer Nunivak (1899–
1901), and Father Jules Jette, S.J. (1910). Once again, there are only
passing remarks except in the case of Father Jette, Mr. Prevost, and
Lieut. Cantwell.

   After 1867, the Saakił Hut'aane Koyukon, Nendaaghe Hut'aane
Koyukon, Too Loghe Hut'aane Koyukon, Too Tleekk'e Hut'aane,
Di'haįį Gwich'in, and Taghe Chox Xut'ana Lower Tanana were
already dislocated from their former territories and the survivors of
all these groups intermarried and were absorbed by the neighboring
groups. The Nendaaghe Hut'aane Koyukon and Too Loghe Hut'aane
Koyukon, also known as K'iitł'it Gwich'in (G), took over the former
territory of the Taghe Chox Xut'ana Lower Tanana and renamed
themselves Denyee Hut'aane Koyukon; the remainder stayed in the
Koyukuk River valley as the Too Loghe Hut'aane (until they, in
turn, were absorbed by the lower Koyukuk groups); others joined
various Gwich'in groups. The Di'haįį Gwich'in were absorbed into
the Neets'aįį, Gwichyaa and Hantee Gwich'in and some went farther
east to join the Teetł'it Gwich'in (G) in Canada. The Taghe Chox
Xut'ana Lower Tanana were absorbed by the Gwichyaa Gwich'in
and the incoming Too Loghe Hut'aane Koyukon.

   These early accounts are supported by the oral histories of the
Koyukon, Iñupiat, Lower Tanana, and Gwich'in peoples. Without
the oral accounts of the native people involved there would be no
history of the Saakił Hut'aane Koyukon, Nendaaghe Hut'aane
Koyukon, Too Loghe Hut'aane Koyukon, Too Tleekk'e Hut'aane,
Di'haįį Gwich'in, and Taghe Chox Xut'ana Lower Tanana people.
Some of these people, in alphabetical order, are Alexander of Kanuti
River, Arctic John Etalook, Catherine Attla, Isabell Charlie, Sarah
Shaaghan Dik, Lucy Frank, Johnny Frank, Sarah Frank, Kilbourn
George, Chief Henry, Moses Henzie, Henry John, Sophie John, Silas
John, Leonard John, Peter John of Minto, Eliza Jones, Bertha Moses,
Simon Paneak, Sophie Paul, Peter and Soozan John of Arctic Village,
Katherine and Steven Peter, Sr., Joshua Rulland, Joe Sun, Edwin
Simon, Isaac Tritt, Henry Williams of Chalkytsik, and all the elders

of the NANA and Arctic Slope regional corporations.

Thanks go also to those who have worked in this region in the last 100 years, especially to Herbert Alexander, Douglas D. Anderson, Ernest S. Burch, Jr., John M. Campbell, Annette McFadyen Clark, Donald W. Clark, John P. Cook, Frederica de Laguna, Robert Gal, S. Craig Gerlach, J. L. Giddings, Nicholas J. Gubser, Frederick Hadleigh-West, Edwin S. Hall, Jr., Helge Ingstad, William N. Irving, Michael Kunz, Robert A. McKennan, Craig W. Mishler, Alexander Hunter Murray, William Schneider, Kenneth M. Schoenberg, F. C. Schrader, Doctor John Simpson, Grant Spearman, James Van Stone, and others. Special thanks go to E. S. Burch, Jr. and Craig Gerlach for reading and re-reading rough drafts; to Dr. Robert Rausch for an excellent editing job; to Rose Speranza for her patient help in the research of this project; and to Dr. James M. Kari for his encouragement and support.

PART I

Koyukon, Gwich'in and Lower Tanana

Koyukon, Gwich'in
and Lower Tanana

The prehistory of the Saakił Hut'aane Koyukon, Nendaaghe Hut'aane Koyukon, Too Loghe Hut'aane Koyukon, Too Tleekk'e Hut'aane, Di'hąįį Gwich'in, and Taghe Chox Xut'ana Lower Tanana is a unique look into the history of the central Brooks Range. This history is taken from the vantage point of early documents and the oral traditon of the Koyukon, Gwich'in, Lower Tanana, and the Iñupiat[*] communities involved. They no longer exist as separate nations. This is the first time that interrelations among these nations have been studied by themselves. So little was known about those nations because they were disbanded and dispersed by the mid 1860s. Indeed, even to arrive at their exact names took research into pre-existing oral sources and new oral sources, not to mention early documents. Except for the Di'hąįį Gwich'in, the Saakił Hut'aane Koyukon, Nendaaghe Hut'aane Koyukon, and Too Loghe Hut'aane Koyukon and the Too Tleekk'e Hut'aane and Taghe Chox Xut'ana Lower Tanana have never been written about as separate groups. Ernest S. Burch, Jr. referred to the Too Loghe Hut'aane[1], but it was not until the present author contacted Catherine Attla[2] of

---

[*] The words Gwich'in, Koyukon, Iñupiat, and Lower Tanana will not be followed anywhere in this text with an "s" because the plurals are incorporated into the meaning of the words themselves. Gwich'in means "people" or "dwellers of." Iñupiat is the plural of Iñupiaq, the singular. I shall not use an "s" on Koyukon or Lower Tanana.

Huslia, Alaska and consulted the Koyukon Athabascan Dictionary manuscript[3] that the Too Loghe Hʉt'aane Koyukon* could be associated with the South Fork band. The Too Loghe Hʉt'aane Koyukon were labeled as the South Fork Band by Annette McFayden Clark.[4] The Nendaaghe and Saakił Hʉt'aane Koyukon, Taghe Chox Xut'ana Lower Tanana and the Too Tleekk'e Hʉt'aane were previously unidentified groups. With reference to the Taghe Chox Xut'ana Lower Tanana, only the early writings of Alexander Hunter Murray, the Hudson's Bay Company trader who established Fort Yukon in 1847, mentioned them as "Tecounka." More recently Shepard Krech, III,[5] mentioned them by the same name and stated they were a Koyukon band; they are also mentioned in Katherine Arndt.[6] Other explorers and the Rev. Robert McDonald of the Anglican Church Missionary Society wrote about them by other names. It was through conversations with Isabell Charlie[7] of Minto, Alaska, that we arrived at Taghe Chox. A later telephone interview with Peter John of Minto, Alaska, fleshed out a real group known as the Taghe Chox Xut'ana or Xut'anayi† Lower Tanana.[8] The Di'haįį Gwich'in have long been alluded to in academic literature—first by Robert McKennan[9] then by Frederick Hadleigh-West[10]—but again no one has written specifically about the Di'haįį Gwich'in, except for Ernest S. Burch, Jr.[11] and Craig W. Mishler.[12] The history of the Saakił, Nendaaghe, and Too Loghe Hʉt'aane Koyukon, and the Too Tleekk'e Hʉt'aane, Di'haįį Gwich'in, and Taghe Chox Xut'ana Lower Tanana has been pieced together from fragments of information both written and oral.

I will begin by settling on some terms for purposes of our discussion then I shall proceed to delineate the estate and range of the Koyukon, Gwich'in, Lower Tanana, and the Iñupiat, which are the larger communities with whom these nations interacted. Then we shall home in on the Saakił, Nendaaghe, and Too Loghe Hʉt'aane

---

* I have added the larger group name to each nation to avoid confusion.
† Xut'ana singular, Xut'anayi plural form.

Koyukon, and the Too Tleekk'e Hut'aane, Di'haii Gwich'in, and
Taghe Chox Xut'ana Lower Tanana delineating the estate and range
of each nation within the larger communities. We shall then follow
their displacement and the subsequent history of each group
individually.

The question of terms arises for a number of reasons. The first
issue concerns names for the groups: should they be called societies,
regional groups, tribes, bands, territories, or nations? This is a
particularly important question given the hunting and gathering
groups involved. The Iñupiat, according to Burch, refer to their
territories as nunqatigiich, which translates to "nations" or
"countries."[13] Nations would apply to the Gwich'in, Koyukon, and
Lower Tanana nations as well in that they regarded themselves as
having "domain over separate territories, their citizens thought of
themselves as being separate peoples, and they engaged one another
in war and in trade."[14] I shall use the term "nations" for all the Iñupiat
entities with exception of the Kaŋianiġmiut, Killiġmiut, and
Qaŋmaliġmiut who have been described as regional bands of the
Kuukpiġmiut.[15] Regardless of the small numbers of people involved
I shall use the term "nations," predominantly, but also use "bands,"
and "groups."

The second area of terms is what Burch calls estate and range
which he explains: "An estate is defined as the geographic area
claimed by a set of individuals to be their property, whereas a range
is the country through which some or all of those individuals actually
travel."[16] This is an especially important distinction since, for
example, the range of the Di'haii Gwich'in was very large (from the
Beaufort Sea to the Yukon River), but the main part of their estate
was by comparison a lot smaller (the upper Koyukuk River). I shall
use estate and range. Boundaries and borders seem to pose another
sticky point, as "boundary" is used solely to refer to the outer limits
of a social system, such as a society. "Border," on the other hand,
refers to the outer limits of a unit of land (i.e., of a territory).[17] Since
we shall be discussing hunter-gatherers, the term "territory" will

also be applied. Having established these terms, I shall begin with the delineation of Koyukon estate and range.

The Koyukon

The Koyukon Indians or the Tl'eeyegge Hʉt'aane Koyukon (indigenous people) are an Athabascan-speaking group of nations that occupy the middle Yukon River[18] from just above the present-day community of Grayling, Alaska, all the way to the present-day community of Beaver, Alaska on the Yukon, and to the south along the lower Tanana River, and the north side of Denaalee [(K) Denali].* To the north their range extended up the Koyukuk River to its headwaters. These are the current perimeters of the Koyukon-speaking area as of 1982.[19] Annette McFadyen-Clark outlined very much the same territory.[20] The Koyukon boundaries and borders have not always been the same; they have changed over the last two hundred years. These changes in estate and range have been brought on by a number of variables, such as changes in the weather, internal and external warfare, famine, disease, changing demands for trade items, change in economy, movement of people, and cataclysmic events. Most of these changes have occurred in the history of the Koyukon nations since 1800. Our area of concern here is the Koyukon people of the upper Kobuk, Noatak, Colville, and Koyukuk rivers. The people of the upper Koyukuk River were known as the Yoonegge Hʉt'aane Koyukon[21] by the Koyukon people who lived along the Yukon River (Fig. 1).

Frederick Whymper, in 1867, described the Koyukon-speaking border and range thus: "The Co-Yukon is the largest tribe on the Yukon River, and extends virtually from the confluence of the Co-Yukuk [Koyukuk] River to Nuclukayette [Noochu Logheyet,] "at the end of the big island."[22] at the junction of the Tanana with the Yukon; for, although some of the intervening tribes have local names, yet they speak one dialect, and may fairly be considered as one

---

* Koyukon name for Mt. McKinley.

Fig. 1. Contemporary Koyukon language speaking area, 2000.

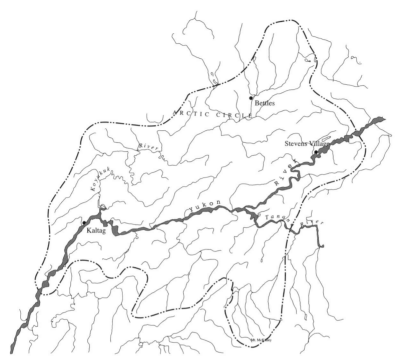

people. They also inhabit the banks of the Co-Yukuk, and other Interior rivers."[23] However, on his map on the inside cover (Fig. 2), he shows the "Newicargut Indianer" as being separate from the Lower Tanana nation whom he called "Tanana Indianer (Gens de Butte)." He goes on later, "Hither come Indians from all quarters, Co-Yukons, Newicarguts, Tananas, and even the Kotch-à-Kutchins from Fort Yukon."[24] This would suggest that Whymper may have thought the Koyukon nations ended at Newicargut (Nowitna River) on the Yukon River. William H. Dall, who traveled with Whymper, described the Koyukon-speaking territory thus: "Lastly, the Western Tinneh, who occupy the region west of the Yukon and the banks of that river below Nuklukayét. They form their tribal designation by the addition of the word "tána," another modification of Tinneh."[25]

McDonald made a trip in 1870 from Fort Yukon to St. Michael,

Fig. 2. Whymper's 1867 drawing of Alaska Native groups up the Yukon.
Courtesy of the Alaska and Polar Regions Archives, Rasmuson Library,
University of Alaska Fairbanks.

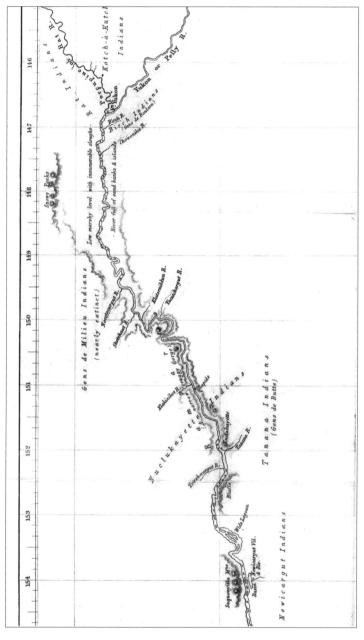

Alaska on Norton Sound and back. While at Niuklukaüt (The Nuklukayèt of Dall and Nuclukayette of Whymper) McDonald described the Koyukon thus: "There are a few of the Tètsi-kutchin [Gwich'in ethnonym for Koyukon people] here. All the Indians assembled here, some from farther down the river, speak as the Tètsi-kutchin [Koyukon], with only a slight difference of dialect..."[26] After leaving Nulato he "Came to two camps of Indians this afternoon they are called Yolikuk Indians [Deg Hit'an]. They all have the features of the Esquimaux, and have their hair cut close on the crown of the head. They speak the same language as the Tètsi-kutchin, with a slight difference."[27] That pretty much concurs with Dall and Whymper. Frederica de Laguna was of the same opinion in 1947.[28] In general that is a rough estimate of Koyukon speaking territory as of 1867–1870.

The Western Borders

Our first task is to establish the western perimeters of Koyukon range around Nulato and the Koyukuk River by using historical documents and interjecting oral accounts. In 1838, Petr V. Malakhov of the Russian-American Company was the first to reach the "Koyukuk"[29] and according to Lieutenant Zagoskin, Malakhov had dealings with the Takyaksa people (Koyukon people).[30] The word Koyukuk was not the local name for the river, but a general word for "river" in Chnagmyut, a coastal luaguage (Cinarmiut, coastal dwellers[31]). Zagoskin called the Koyukon "InKilik" (Ingalik, he did not distinguish between the Ingalik and the Koyukon[32]) and delineated the southwestern extent of the Ingalik people when he wrote "The Inkilik people who live along the Yukon from the mouth of the Chagelyuk [Shagaluk Slough] to Nulato have adopted the dress of the coast..."[33] Zagoskin was the first to have written about the Koyukon Indian in the Middle Yukon in the vicinity of Nulato and up the Koyukuk River to the mouth of the present-day Kateel River in March of 1843. Here he found a small community that he called Khotylakaket (Kodeel Kkaakk'et) village and whose inhabitants he called "the Inkilik of the Yunnaka-Khotana" (people of the Yunnaka) after the name of the river which was called the Yunnaka River (Koyukuk River).[34] The present spelling for the Yunneka-Khotana or "upland people" and the Yunnaka River is Yoonegge Hʉt'aane Koyukon and Yoonegge River. This is the name given to the Koyukuk River people by those Koyukon who lived along the Yukon River.

Hʉt'aane is variously spelled *hʉt'aane*, *hʉt'aana* (two dialect variants), and *khotana* (old spelling) and means "dwellers of" in the Koyukon language (*xut'ana* and plural *xut'anayi* in Lower Tanana and *gwich'in* in Gwich'in). Kkʉyetl'ots'en Hʉt'aane Koyukon is another name for "people of the upper Koyukuk River."[35] Zagoskin could not go further north for his guide was only a boy and no one in the village would take him up the river since they were on their way to the spring caribou hunt. Besides, they explained, "the snow is soft and deep."[36]

However, Zagoskin was a very fortunate man in finding a very good informant in the old man, Kitsykaka [Magpie (K'ets'eggaagge')[37]] (K), who commanded special respect among his kinsmen because of his wealth and large household.[38] K'ets'eggaagge' was evidently a community leader. He was also a well-known medicine man.[39] The old man told him "that there is a river in the extreme north, Tutlẻka-khotana or Tyneka-khutana,[40] and that the people living along its upper waters have direct contact with the Naleygmyut [generally Inupiat speakers]." The people living on the south coast of Norton Bay call this river Chilivik[41] (de Laguna translated the same passage as "Tulika-hotena or Tine-ka-hotena").[42]

Both Zagoskin and the editors of the 1967 issue of his book asserted that the Chilivik is the Selawik River (Siilivik) but the present name, in Koyukon, for Selawik River people is Nozaat No' Hʉt'aane (K) and the present name for people of the Kobuk River is Hʉlghaatne Hʉt'aane (K); the area of the Noatak is known as Nendaaghe.[43] The name for themselves is not known, but there is a clue. The area of the upper Noatak River is called Nendaaghe

(Moving Spirit[44]) in Koyukon. This is not the name for the Noatak River—just for the area of the upper Noatak River.[45] The residents of the area would be known as Nendaaghe Hut'aane Koyukon. Those names do not correspond with Zagoskin's names. The people of Kodeel Kkaakk'et village drew maps for Zagoskin but he was not aware of the Kobuk at the time and the "extreme north" certainly was not the headwaters of the Kateel River. It is more likely that the river in the "extreme north" was the Colville River since the people at its headwaters did have direct contact with the Iñupiat (Naleygmyut). In any case by Koyukon standards the distance between the Siilivik (Selawik River) and the mouth of the Kateel River is not extreme. Furthermore, the word *khotana (hut'aane, hut'aana)* at the end of the words suggests a group name and not the name of a river such as the Siilivik (Selawik).

Some light can be shed upon the subject if we look at the names as group names instead of place names: Tutleka-Khotana or Tyneka-Khotana. If we look at the early writing of Koyukon and Gwich'in names in general, there is a tendency to use "k," "t," or "r" in place of "gh", "g," or "gw" and "d." Tutleka-Khotana is not far removed then from Too Tleekk'e Hut'aane[46] meaning "summit water."[47] The Too Tleekk'e Hut'aane are described by Jette as being the local band of Koyukon at Olsons Lake at the headwaters of the Ray, Dall, and Kanuti rivers. This name went out of usage between 1910 and the present. No one living presently can recall the Too Tleekk'e Hut'aane name. That was a very specific localized group. Talowa,[48] located near Olsons Lake, is also the location of a massacre which occurred about 1851. The community of Talowa is referred to as Too Loghe by the people of Allakaket.[49] The survivors were reported to have shifted "permanently to Neeltugh Tene, near the mouth of the South Fork of the Koyukuk."[50]

One survivor of that incident was Alexander,[51] the father of Big William, Big Beatus, Linus, and South Fork Henry.[52] Alexander was a Gwich'in person[53] which brings into question who the residents of Too Loghe (aka Talowa) were in 1851 and who the perpetrators might have been. The only known surviving residents were Gwich'in, but it might have been a mixed Too Loghe Hʉt'aane Koyukon and Di'haii Gwich'in community. The perpetrators were most likely the Menhtee Xut'ana[*] Lower Tanana (Minto Flats), who occupied the the Lower Tanana River, and the Shahnyaati' band of the Gwichyaa Gwich'in known as the Deenduu Gwich'in. Several of Alexander's family members were taken to the Yukon River after the massacre. In one story it was his mother and sister; in another telling it was his two brothers.[54] Perhaps it was both, for they were taken to the vicinity of Stevens Village and raised by a foster father. Their mother died there. Stevens Village did not exist until 1902;[55] instead there was a community at the mouth of the Dall River called Tehlalu-chaket or Tchtau-ch-ket.[56] The present spelling is Hʉdochaaget[57] meaning "the mouth of the opening" or "river mouth."[58]

The place name and settlement name "Too Loghe," of Olsons Lake, has survived as Too Loghe Hʉt'aane Koyukon, a much broader phrase for the Koyukuk headwaters people as reported by the people of Allakaket. Too Tleekk'e Hʉt'aane has long ago gone out of usage since no one lived at Olsons Lake after the massacre (circa 1851). I hesitate at this point to identify the Too Tleekk'e Hʉt'aane as Koyukon people because, as I noted above, the only known survivor was Alexander, a Gwich'in Indian. This may have been the earliest, oldest, and only Koyukon ethnonym for the Di'haii Gwich'in people. Too Loghe Hʉt'aane Koyukon is the name for the present day people of the South Fork band.[59] The Too Loghe Hʉt'aane Koyukon are (1) the "headwaters people," (2) the South Fork band, (3) the Yoonegge Hʉt'aane Koyukon, (4) the K'iitł'it Gwich'in,[60] and (5) the Kkʉyetl'ots'en Hʉt'aane Koyukon. Kkʉyetl'ots'en Hʉt'aane Koyukon is another name for "people of the upper Koyukuk River." It literally means "toward the head of willow river,"[61] K'uytl'ohutana (willow headwaters people) in Lower Tanana.[62] K'iitł'it, in Gwich'in, means "headwaters of the K'ii River" (Birch River) and it is also the

---

* What the Minto Flats people call themselves—Menhtee Xut'ana.

Gwich'in place name for Anaktuvuk Pass. Burch has suggested the similarity between the two names is very close. K'iitł'it and Kkuyetl'ot are very similar; the former is the headwaters of the Birch River (Gwich'in) and the latter of the Willow River (Koyukon). Both are names for the Koyukuk River.

We know the Too Loghe Hut'aane Koyukon did not speak Gwich'in, for when McDonald set Sahtaii (Shaht'aii), Veyilyo (Veeyilyo), Choowhalhzi (Ch'ookhwałzhii), and the K'iitł'it Gwich'in (aka Too Loghe Hut'aane Koyukon) in March of 1867 at the Neets'aii Gwich'in* camp, he reported that "All the Indians assembled here, some from farther down the river, speak as the Tètsi-kutchin (Koyukon), with only a slight difference of dialect..."[63] From this information we can gather that the Too Loghe Hut'aane Koyukon spoke Koyukon.

If we pursue the group-name theory, then what about Tyneka-khotana? The Koyukon suffix *negge* is a general term meaning "up land, away from the main river," as in *donegge* or *yoonegge*. *Tyneka* is *donegge*. The alternate spelling for Too Loghe Hut'aane Koyukon is Too Loghe Hut'anekka Koyukon[64] which could account for some confusion—Hut'anekka, meaning *hut'aane* "dwellers of" and *kkaa*, "more than one." Thus Tyneka or Donegge Hut'aane means "people who live farther up the river than where the speaker is." Tutḻeka-Khotana or Tyneka-Khotana are the Too Tleekk'e Hut'aane and the Donegge kkaa Hut'aane Koyukon. That is more than one group of Koyukon above the Kodeel Kkaakk'e estate, plus the Too Tleekk'e Hut'aane. The first group, Too Tleekk'e Hut'aane, was massacred at Too Loghe on Olsons Lake in 1851 and the survivors were reported to have moved to the South Fork (Neek'ilahno',[65] Neek'elehno'[66])† Koyukuk River and definately to the Yukon River near the Dall River.

---

* Gwich'in nation to the east of the Di'haii Gwich'in.

† Neek'elehno' means "something (salmon) stops (to spawn) river." The words in parenthesis are understood in the meaning of the whole word. I will use Neek'elehno' since it is the latest spelling of the word.

K'ets'eeggaagge' was very clear, the Too Tleekk'e Hut'aane and the Donegge kkaa Hut'aane, i.e. plural groups up the river. There were at least two separate nations at the time of Zagoskin's 1842 visit to the lower Koyukuk River.

Zagoskin went on with notes for future explorers and traders:

> For a long way as you go up this river there are no people at all with the exception of a trail house situated half a day's journey from Khotylkakat [Kodeel Kkaakk'et]; on the upper reaches of the river, however, where it has many tributaries, there are a good many natives. They also belong to the tribe of the Ttynay [Denaa]. Nevertheless they differ from their downriver fellow tribesmen in speech, and they have no shamans; and they live in widely separated families in the mountains, where they hunt deer, sable, wolverine, and fox. Beaver and otter are not very plentiful in their country. Parties of them come down each spring from the upper river to Khotylkaket [Kodeel Kkaakk'et] and to the mouth of the Yunnaka to trade their furs for tobacco, beads, and ironware. On the return trip some of them prefer to take the route up the Yuna (the Yukon).[67]

In all, Zagoskin came across ten Yoonegge Hut'aane Koyukon villages and one large settlement of summer houses on the Notaglita River (Beaver Creek)[68] with a total population of 289 and, by this trip, established for our purposes a western boundary for the Kodeel Kkaakk'e Hut'aane Koyukon[69] (Kateel River nation), the headwaters of the Kateel River.

It is not clear from Zagoskin's report what the northern and western boundaries of the Yoonegge Hut'aane Koyukon were. All the communities were on the lower Koyukuk River valley, the Kateel and Dulbi rivers, and Dulbi Slough at the time.[70] It so happened that sometime during the 1820s and 1830s a section of the Koyukuk River (probably below Kanuti River) was vacated because it had been over-fished and the inhabitants moved along the Yukon for a

period of time.[71] It is my opinion that, if the Yoonegge Hʉt'aane
Koyukon went to the Yukon River above the mouth of the Koyukuk
River, then they probably went west into the upper Kobuk and east
to the Chandalar River or to the Lower Ramparts* along the Yukon
River between the Dall River and the confluence of the Tanana and
Yukon rivers as well. Burch suggested the possibility of the central
Koyukuk River being "devoid of human inhabitants,"[72] during this
same period. According to dendrochronological studies conducted
by J. L. Giddings, the weather in northwestern Alaska was colder
during the 1820s and 1830s.[73] That may have effected the availability
of subsistence resources since, generally speaking, colder conditions
pose a hardship upon animal life. Fish was, and is, a major food
source for the Koyukon and without it they faced starvation. The
people who remained along that section of the river (probably
between the Kanuti and Kateel rivers) starved.[74] The northern
boundaries of the Koyukon nation could not be clearly established
by Zagoskin, but he was satisfied to have found proof that the
Koyukon traded to the Naleygmut[75] (generally Iñupiat speakers).
McFadyen Clark amplifies this point further for Hotham Inlet,
"Occasionally, a Koyukuk trader accompanied his Kobuk partner to
the major Inupiat fair at Hotham Inlet on Kotzebue Sound."[76]

From our examination we have discovered that there were at
least two Koyukon nations (maybe three) on the Koyukuk River in
1843: mainly the Kodeel Kkaakk'e Hʉt'aane Koyukon of the Kateel
River, the Donegge kkaa Hʉt'aane Koyukon (plural groups at the
headwaters), and an unidentified group known as the Too Tleekk'e
Hʉt'aane of the Olsons Lake region. As discussed earlier, we are not
sure whether they were Koyukon or Gwich'in as we have their
ethnonym only from the Koyukon perspective. Van Stone and
Goddard had the lower Koyukuk occupied by the "Yunnaka Khotana"
[Yoonegge Hʉt'aane Koyukon (to reiterate, a Yukon River Koyukon

---

* The Lower Ramparts between the confluence of the Tanana and Yukon rivers and
the Dall River. The Upper Ramparts begin just above Circle, Alaska.

name for the Koyukuk River people)] and an "unnamed Koyukon group," above that for the rest of the Koyukuk River valley (Fig. 3).[77]

Our next positive identification of the Koyukon is by Captain Rochfort Maguire and his ship's surgeon, Doctor John Simpson, who wintered aboard the *HMS Plover* at Point Barrow, Alaska in 1852–1854 in search of Sir John Franklin. Dr. John Simpson was fluent in Iñupiaq and made their stay more productive and amenable.[78] Dr. Simpson's map (Fig. 4) shows the extent of the "Mountain Indian Country." Simpson begins his description of the country thus: "The largest and best known rivers are four, all of which take their rise far to the south-east in a mountainous country, inhabited by Indians."[79] He goes on to describe the Colville, Noatak, Kobuk, and Selawik rivers—all of which are occupied at their headwaters by "mountainous Indians." "The inland Esquimaux

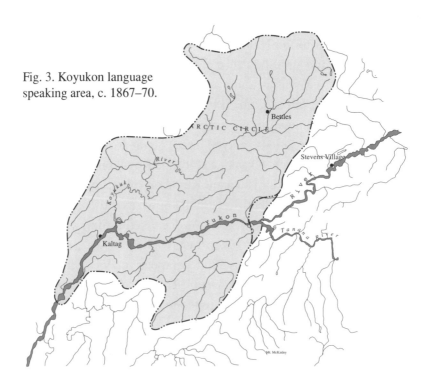

Fig. 3. Koyukon language speaking area, c. 1867–70.

Fig. 4. Koyukuk River estates in 1843. Map created by Karen Farrell and Adeline Raboff.

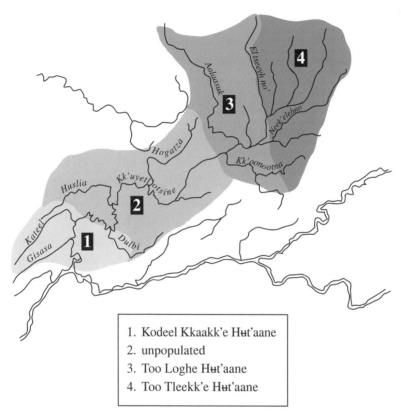

1. Kodeel Kkaakk'e Hʉt'aane
2. unpopulated
3. Too Loghe Hʉt'aane
4. Too Tleekk'e Hʉt'aane

[Ka'ng-ma-li-meun[80] and Nu-na-tan'g-meun[81]] also call them Ko'-yu-kan, and divide them into three sections or tribes, two of which they know, and say they have different modes of dancing. One is called It'-ka-lyi,* and inhabits the It'-ka-ling River [Itkillik River (Indian River)],...the second, It-kal-ya'-run-in, whose country is further south; and the third, whom they have never seen, but only heard of as the people who barter wolverine skins, knives, guns,

---

* "Itqillich refers to both Koyukon and Kutchin, and to all other Indians," Ernest S. Burch, Jr, personal communication, 1999.

and ammunition to the Esquimaux at Herschel Island...."[82] Simpson was cautious about names.[*] The Kuukpiġmiut, the Colville River Iñupiat, knew the first two groups well and called them Ko'-yu-kan. The first group, the It'-kal-ya'-run-in and Ko'-yu-kan, were met by Maguire near the mouth of the Colville River.[83] John Murdoch identified these It-kal-ya'-run-in as the "Rat Indians" whom he identified as the Vunta'-Kūtchin. Furthermore (on the same page), he said that Maguire, "seems to have distributed among them printed 'information slips,' which they immediately carried to Fort Yukon, and returning to the coast with a letter from the clerk in charge, delivered it to Capt. Collison on board of the *Enterprise* at Barter Island, July 18, 1854."[84] The response came from William Lucas Hardisty, Clerk-in-Charge at Fort Youcon (Yukon). Murdoch went on to say that the "The Point Barrow also know the name of the U'na-kho-tana, or En'akotina, as they pronounce it. Their intercourse with all these Indians appears to be rather slight and purely commercial," which in the 1880s was correct. These two groups (Koyukon and Gwich'in) had different ways of dancing that we know to be true. The third group are the Neets'ąįį Gwich'in[85] and/or Vantee/Vuntet Gwich'in[86] who traded frequently with the Iñupiat at Barter Island and Herschel Island.[†] This places the north and northwestern Koyukon boundaries along the upper Kobuk, Noatak, and Colville rivers. As for the northeastern, eastern and southeastern

---

[*] "It is at all times desirable that great caution should be used in drawing inferences from mere sounds in an unwritten language which is but partially known, yet it seems worthy of remark, that the Esquimaux word, *kōk*, a river, prefixed to the name Yu-kon, will bear a strong resemblance to the name Ko'-yu'kon, given them to the Indians inhabiting the country through which the You-con flows." Simpson in Maguire, 1988: 544.

You-con is a Gwich'in word. The first part of the word, *you* or *yu* is a very old stem or contraction of a longer phrase which is a reference to the great distance the river travels. The second part of the word, *con* or *kon* is a large body of moving water. My great aunt Belle Stevens Luke referred to herself as Kaii youcon.

[†] The Gwich'in place names for Barter Island and Herschel Island are Łeeridiidàl and Nanjuughat.

borders and boundaries we can only guess at this point. For the present we shall continue our reconstruction of the Koyukon western borders moving from south to north, however, I shall omit the Siiḷviim Kañianiġmiut,[87] the upper Siilivik (Selawik River) Iñupiaq nation, and begin with the Kobuk River (Fig. 5).

THE KOBUK RIVER SOURCES

Lieut. George M. Stoney of the U. S. Navy was one of the first Euro-Americans up the Kobuk River (1885–86).[88] He wrote of the upper Kobuk natives in particular, "Long ago they were undoubtedly closely allied to the natives of the Koyukuk River; because the oldest natives of the Putnam [Kobuk] valley still speak that language and say that their fathers knew no other."[89] The upper Kobuk River people were Koyukon. Burch, who has combined written and oral accounts in his most recent publication, *The Iñupiaq Eskimo Nations of*

Fig. 5. Dr. John Simpson's map of 1854 showing "mountainous Indian country". Courtesy of Rare Book Manuscripts & Special Collections, Duke University.

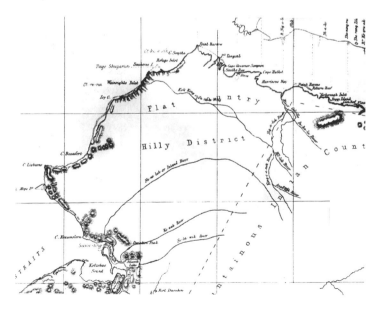

Northwest Alaska, 1998, addresses the upper Kobuk River valley in his chapter about the Kuuvaum Kaŋiaġmiut Iñupiat.* He confirms Stoney's report.

For the Kobuk River Burch writes:

> It now seems increasingly clear that, during the first half of the nineteenth century, the inhabitants of the upper Kobuk district were Koyukon-speaking Indians specifically. The Iñupiaq-Koyukon border was then in the Kobuk valley, apparently just below the mouth of the Kogoluktuk River, not on the Kobuk-Koyukuk divide. The upper Kobuk-Koyukon probably constituted a distinct nation of Koyukon speakers because of the distance between them and their relatives on the Koyukuk River. On the other hand, the divide between the two valleys is easy to cross, and they may have been a regional band of the main Koyukon population. Their own name for themselves has been lost. They may have been called Qalamiut by the Iñupiaq neighbors, after their primary village at Qala.[90]

Then again, the late Robert Nasruk Cleveland (born 1883) "told [Don Charles] Foote that Indians or Indian-like people had lived in the upper Kobuk valley not very long before his time. In one passage he said that they had extended from Walker Lake, near the Kobuk headwaters, down to the mouth of the Kogoluktuk River,..."[91] Burch goes on to say, "During the second half of the nineteenth century, and specifically between about 1850 and 1880, the upper Kobuk-Koyukon became assimilated by the Iñupiat."[92] It is apparent that the Kogoluktuk River was a border with the Akuniġmiut Iñupiat (central Kobuk River nation), but it remains to be seen which

---

* The subject is covered much more thoroughly in Burch, Ernest S., Jr., Eliza Jones, Hannah P. Loon, Lawrence D. Kaplan, "The Ethnogenesis of the Kuuvaum Kaŋiaġmiut." *Ethnohistory* 46, no. 2, (1999).

Koyukon nation shared that border.

If we review, Chief* Henry[93] reported that during the 1820s and 1830s the Koyukon people abandoned the Koyukuk River valley and moved to the Yukon River. This may have been brought on by a combination of fewer caribou and fish. If the Yoonegge Hʉt'aane Koyukon (the Koyukuk River people) abandoned the Koyukuk River, then the Yukon River is not the only place that they would have moved to. Burch posited that the Koyukuk River was virtually uninhabited during and after the period of Zagoskin's visit in 1842,[94]

Fig. 6. 1800 map of the Nendaaghe, Saakił, and Too Loghe Koyukon estates. Map created by Karen Farrell and Adeline Raboff.

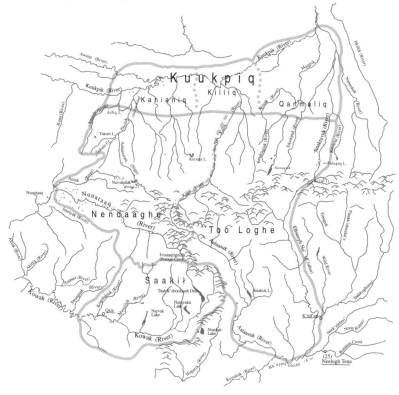

* Chief Henry, also known as Bekk'oyoodaałdleede which means "his arrow doesn't miss," Eliza Jones, personal communication, 1999.

which certainly was the case. If the Yoonegge Hʉt'aane Koyukon moved out of the Koyukuk River because of famine, they would have moved north, south, east, and west, in short, anywhere they knew of relatives and some source of food. The upper Kobuk River valley would have been an ideal place, given that the Yoonegge Hʉt'aane Koyukon already had relatives there. The Kogoluktuk River is an Iñupiat/Koyukon boundary, but the name of the Koyukon nation which occupied the upper Kobuk valley is not known. One of the place names of the upper Kobuk is Saakiłhutaane.[95] The person who named that place was Kituq, one of the last Koyukon men in the upper Kobuk.[96] He was an old man when Jenny Masruana Jackson, born 1893, of Kobuk village was a young girl. Kituq spoke Koyukon and Iñupiat fluently and no doubt was there when Cantwell and Stoney passed through the country in 1885–1886. Saakiłhutaane is a group name. As we discussed earlier *hʉt'aane*, *hʉt'aana*, and *khotana* all mean "dwellers of" in Koyukon. The word *saakiłhutaane* means "flat piece of ground."[97] However, *saakił* is unintelligible in contemporary Koyukon.[98] *Saa* in upper Kobuk River Iñupiat means "something thin," as in "a thin flat layer of ice," but the *kił* part of the word is not intelligible.[99] This could have been a band name that fell out of usage at an earlier time in which case it would have been Saakił Hʉt'aane Koyukon.* The contemporary Koyukon name for the people of the Kobuk River is Hʉlghaatne Hʉt'aane (K) (dweller of the oily area river). The Kogoluktuk River was an Akuniġmiut Iñupiat/Saakił Hʉt'aane Koyukon border. We may get a clearer picture of this border if we turn to a few oral accounts.

We will begin with the oral history of the late Joe Immałuuraq Sun, born 1900,[100] from the upper Kobuk River area. Immałuuraq traced his paternal lineage to the Qalamiu[101] (also Qalamiut, the plural

---

* I will use Saakił Hʉt'aane Koyukon to distinguish between upper Kobuk Koyukon and the Nendaaghe Hʉt'aane Koyukon. I use quotation marks to show that no one know for sure what the upper Kobuk River Koyukon were called. Some pieces of information are lost; those who would have known are no longer alive.

of Qalamiu) who resided along the upper Kobuk River above the confluence of the Maniïḷaq River.[102] The settlement of Qala was a few miles above the present day community of Kobuk, Alaska.[103] The Qalamiut, he said, "were always said to be able to speak the Indian tongue because they were the descendants of Indians. That is why the Kuuvaŋmiut, people of the Kobuk, were always referred to as Itqïḷïaġruch, 'Indian.' They are hardly called that anymore because those who knew about it are all gone now. They called them Itqïḷïaġruch because they descended from the Indians."[104] The Iñupiat of Anaktuvuk Pass also referred to the Kobuk Iñupiat as Itkilliruich,[105] which means Indian in their dialect.

Immaḷuuraq's paternal grandfather was called Aŋarraaq,[106] his grandmother's first husband. What is significant is the name Aŋarraaq, which appears among the Koyukon and the Neets'ąįį Gwich'in of the Chandalar River as well. Aŋarraaq, I believe, is a name that originated in the upper Kobuk River. That the name shows up east of the upper Kobuk suggests eastward movement of the Koyukon population at some time in the past. However, no one among the Iñupiat, Koyukon, or Gwich'in, whom I have asked, seems to know what the name means. "It's just a name," is the common response. My conclusion about the name is that it demonstrates prolonged contact among the Kobuk River Iñupiat—both Akuniġmiut Iñupiat (central Kobuk) and Kuuvaum Kaŋiaġmiut Iñupiat (upper Kobuk)—and the Saakił, Nendaaghe, and Too Loghe Hʉt'aane Koyukon.

Immaḷuuraq and Charlie Pigliġiaq Custer (born circa 1870)[107] related a war story between the Akuniġmiut Iñupiat of the central Kobuk and a group of Indians called Iyaġaaġmiut, independently of each other and at different times. Charlie Pigliġiaq Custer was Immaḷuuraq's cousin on his mother's side (Fig. 7). The elder of the two was Pigliġiaq. The battle ranged from the Salmon, Maniïḷaq, Nunataaq (Noatak), and the upper Aalaasuk[108] (Alatna) rivers. The Salmon River is below the Kogoluktuk River and the Maniïḷaq River is above the Kogoluktuk River, the Kogoluktuk River being the

Fig. 7. Charlie Pigliġiaq Custer and Joe Immałuuraq Sun family tree.*

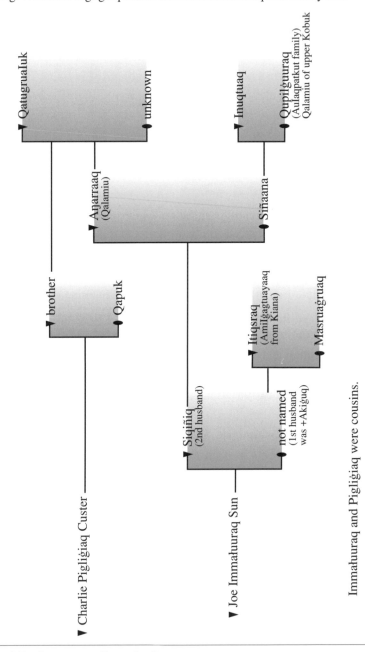

* Family tree according to Joe Sun.

border and boundary along the upper Kobuk River between the
Akuniġmiut Iñupiat and the Saakił Hut'aane Koyukon. Since this is
a long story I will take excerpts from both stories and paraphrase
sections of the text. Since Pigliġiaq is the elder of the two, this telling
will favor his rendition:

SAYYEN (ALSO KNOWN AT SAÏTYAT)

Sayyen came into the central Kobuk River area, around
Salmon River, when he was a young man and he stayed
with an Iñupiat family. He was raised with their son whose
name was Qatïya'aana. Qatïya'aana became like a brother
to him. Later on when he became a man he moved to the
Nunataaq (Noatak) area where he was reported to have
relatives. He acquired two wives. Now as an adult and a
member of another group he was obliged to kill Kobuk
hunters who went up into the Nunataaq area to hunt
caribou.

Sayyen returned from time to time to the hills at the
headwaters of the Manïïłaq River, but was living at
Evisaaktinmilik [Ivisaaqtnilik[109] (Portage Creek) Ivisaaq
means "red stone" (ochre)[110]] which is just over the divide
on the Nunataaq side. From there he killed the Iñupiat who
occasionally came up the valley, by ambush. After one
such ambush Sayyen discovered that he had accidentally
killed his foster brother, Qatïya'aana. Sayyen wept.
Sayyen's nephew was with him; his name was Qïvlïuraq.
Qatïya'aana's campanion was called Kataksiñaq. He ran
away without his clothing and traveled down the Manïïłaq
River where he eventually died from exposure. Sayyen
and his companions then headed northward to their
settlement along the upper Nunataaq (Noatak River)
knowing that there would be some retaliation for their
actions. However, they were obliged by custom to stay
away from the community for three days, since they had
killed a man. They were observing this custom not far

from their settlement.

"There was a person named Aakałukpak* amongst the
Salmon River people…He started getting some men
together to travel. As they got a little ways from Salmon
River they came upon a woman and her son, a young man.
So Aakałukpak wanted that boy to go with him, if he
wouldn't he would kill them right there…They were
planning to go to the three people that had killed that
guy (Qatïya'aana). The womans' son's name was
Uularaġuaraq."[111]

The mother of Uularaġuaraq requested that he only use
three arrows. Here it's important to point out that
Immałuuraq said it was because the boy had nothing
against those people, whereas Pigliġiaq said it was because
the boy had one relative who was killed "up that way,"
consequently he must use only three arrows.

When they came to Sayyen's settlement on the Aalaasuk
(Alatna River), they saw the hut of the three men, but they
were not certain that it was their hut because "a long time
ago when a girl reaches puberty they keep her away from
the settlement (or if a woman gives birth[112]) and these
Salmon River guys thought there was a young woman in
that place. So they told Uularaġuaraq, the young man with
only three arrows, to go to that place."[113]

A battle ensued and the only ones left living among the
Indians were a young man, the wounded Sayyen, and his
two wives. "They go over to the Arctic Side of the
mountains. The Kobukers go back home."[114] Sayyen died
later that winter of his wounds. These people were called
Iyġaaaġmiut and they lived at the headwaters of the
Nunataaq (Noatak) and Aalaasuk (Alatna) rivers.

In reviewing the story we find that (1) here, for the first time, is

---

* This is a personal name from the upper Kobuk River, which does not have a
translation, but connotes a very strong man. Thomas Jackson, personal communication,
1999.

the Akuniġmiut Iñupiat or the central Kobuk River Iñupiaq name for the Nendaaghe Hʉt'aane Koyukon, Iyaġaaġmiut (Those who dwell among the rocks), (2) Sayyen came into the central Kobuk area as a young boy and was raised by an Iñupiaq family adapting to their language and customs, (3) that Sayyen spent his formative years along the central Kobuk River, (4) the Iñupiat were very familiar with the Koyukon customs and beliefs, (5) Aakałukpak, an Akuniġmiut Iñupiat man who came from the Salmon River, came to avenge the murder of Qatïya'aana, (6) a young man was abducted and drawn into the war party; he may have been a Saakił Hʉt'aane Koyukon who became Iñupiatized, (7) the Nendaaghe Hʉt'aane Koyukon were mountain people who often traveled to the central and upper Kobuk River, (8) the Nendaaghe and Too Loghe Hʉt'aane Koyukon occupied the upper Nunataaq (Noatak) and Aalaasuk (Alatna) rivers at the earliest known period, (9) that either Sayyen's nephew had an Iñupiaq name or it was a name that had been translated into Iñupiaq, and (10) the upper Kobuk River Saakił Hʉt'aane Koyukon were already starting to be assimilated by the Iñupiat. Tommy Paanikaliaq[115] Douglas (born 1925) of Shungnak, Alaska said that the events in this story took place at Twelve-Mile, Portage Creek. According to Immałuraaq, Sayyen's camp was at Ivasaaqtiġnilik, which is on Portage Creek.[116] The events in this story could have coincided with the abandonment of the middle Koyukuk River in the 1820s and 30s.

The Iyaġaaġmiut were the Nendaaghe Hʉt'aane Koyukon who occupied the upper Nunataaq (Noatak River). The Iñupiat estate of Iyaġaaq is the estate known as Nendaaghe in Koyukon. That is, one specific goup of Koyukon who occupied the upper Noatak were known as the Nendaaghe Hʉt'aane Koyukon and their estate was known as Nendaaghe. The upper Aalaasuk (Alatna River) by contrast was probably occupied by the Too Loghe Hʉt'aane Koyukon, as they constitute the headwaters of the Koyukuk River. The Kobuk River Iñupiat did not differentiate between the Nendaaghe Hʉt'aane Koyukon and the Too Loghe Hʉt'aane Koyukon. They were both known as Iyaġaaġmiut by the Kobuk River Iñupiat.

The same Iyaġaaġmiut are part of a story told by Dikajaw[117] (I), an upper Kobuk River Iñupiaq woman who moved to Allakaket, Alaska[118] after 1900:

> One fall the Kobuk hunters went sheep hunting up the headwaters of the Kobuk and Noatak. They were up there just long enough for everyone to get their share of skins. Then on the return trip when they were loaded down with sheep skins one man and his son got lost out there in the mountains. The other hunters returned to the Kobuk and told the families that they looked for the lost hunters, but finally they had to leave. Their families thought they had lost those two and they were sad.
>
> Meanwhile those hunters built a shelter with the sheep skins. The father made snowshoes, and he tanned all those sheepskins and made clothing for them. They hunted and ate.
>
> Finally it was about February or March, about then, and they just started to walk. After a while they ran into some people. They didn't know how to communicate with them, but they used sign language and they shared food with each other. Somehow, the other people understood that they were lost and an elderly man told them to go in the direction where the sun is setting.
>
> The father and son headed back and it was not until the fall time that they returned to the Kobuk River. Of course, their families were overjoyed to have them back.

Her granddaughter, Bertha Nictune Moses, went on to say, "They think those two were probably over near the Chandalar River when they ran into those Iyaġaaġmiut. That story was told by my grandmother [Dikajaw], but that was before her time. She was born in 1860. Those people had relatives among the Iyaġaaġmiut too. Iyaġaaġmiut, that mean those people live among the rocks. Rocky Mountain people. My grandmother say they used to live up Alatna

River. They got along with the Iyaġaaġmiut, but they didn't get along with the Lower Koyukuk people."

All informants in this instance place the Nendaaghe and Too Loghe Hʉt'aane Koyukon/Iyaġaaġmiut, at the headwaters of the Nunataaq (Noatak) and Aalaasuk (Alatna) rivers. We know from previous information that there was a border at the Kogoluktuk River between the Iñupiat and the upper Kobuk River Saakił Hʉt'aane Koyukon. Immałuuraq located Ivisaaqtiġnilik on Portage Creek along the upper Nunataaq (Noatak River) where Sayyen, the Iyaġaaġmiut (I), died after his last battle with the Akuniġmiut Iñupiat, the central Kobuk River Iñupiat. Immałuuraq also told a similar story about hunters getting lost and I think it is the same story embellished and told from the Kobuk River side.[120] Although we cannot tell for sure it seems that Pigliġiaq and Immałuuraq's story is older than the story of Dikajaw, because by the time of Dikajaw's story, the Iyaġaaġmiut were very much to the east of the upper Nunataaq (Noatak) and Aalaasuk (Alatna) rivers. If Burch is correct in his placement of the Koyukon assimilation in the upper Kobuk River between 1850 and 1880, then Pigliġiaq and Immałuuraq's story must have been before that, quite possibly during the abandonment of the central Koyukuk River* by the Koyukon during the 1820s and 1830s. In Pigliġiaq and Immałuuraq's story the Nendaaghe Hʉt'aane Koyukon and Too Loghe Hʉt'aane Koyukon who lived along the upper Nunataaq came into the Kobuk River area for a short period of time, but their primary residence was in the Noatak and Alatna rivers. I think that it is safe to assume that Sayyen coud not have been the only refugee from the Nunataaq (Noatak). It has been stated that the Nendaaghe Hʉt'aane Koyukon lived year round in the upper Noatak and were closely related to the central and upper Kobuk people.[121] The Dikajaw story is a very nice piece of information, because we can definitely place the lost hunters episode sometime

---

* Central Koyukuk River, between Kateel and Kanuti rivers.

before 1860, and at that time, the Nendaaghe Hut'aane Koyukon had already been gone from Nendaaghe/Iyaġaaq* long enough for the Akuniġmiut Iñupiat to have lost the ability to communicate with them, say a period of at least 10 to 15 years.

There is a distinct possibility that the Nendaaghe Hut'aane Koyukon may have been at war with the upper Kobuk Saakił Hut'aane Koyukon. If that was the case, then the Saakił Hut'aane Koyukon would have appealed to their downriver Iñupiat relatives to help them repel the incursion. This would have hastened the assimilation process. The Koyukon nations were sometimes at war with one another. That two Koyukon nations were at war with each other in the upper Kobuk area in the early nineteenth century can be corroborated by the following story.

This story is relevant to our discussion, but it is told by a Neets'aii Gwich'in informant, the late Johnny Frank (born 1880) of Venetie, whom Robert McKennan† interviewed in 1933. I will take excerpts from the text and paraphrase:

> "Dihch'i'ts'ik‡ (Slender Old Man) and Dinilthoo§ (Blond Whiskers) were powerful shamans who lived long ago; the former was a man who always used his power to help people, but the latter used his to harm them."[122]
> Basically Dinilthoo killed Dihch'its'ik's wives through sorcery and interfered with his efforts to hunt. At last Dihchi'its'ik became fed up and avenged himself by throwing frozen sea water at Dinilthoo. He knew that Dinilthoo did not know anything about sea water and would

---

* Estate of the Iyaġaaġmiut and Nendaaghe Hut'aane Koyukon.

† McKennan, 1965: 61, "The natsai, on the other hand, came to the Chandalar from the Kobuk River, following along the Brooks Range and traversing the territory of the Dihai Kutchin." McKennan was grossly confused in this account where he ties the phratry lines to movements of people. However, the fact that he established this movement, at a time when the informants were closer to the events is significant.

‡ Gwich'in words written into contemporary orthography by Adeline Peter Raboff.

§ Although this can also be Dinilts'oo, I will use Dinilthoo since this is a dialect difference. Johnny Frank's language was peppered with Di'haii Gwich'in words.

be defenseless against it. "The latter did not feel the blow, but shortly after ward he began to feel cold although it was the height of the mosquito season. Dinilthoo and his wives went to their tent and built a huge fire, but the shaman continued to shiver as though it was the dead of winter." Dinilthoo and his wives died.

"There was an Eskimo woman on the Kobuk who was a powerful shaman." She was also dealt with by Dihch'i'ts'ik.

Then, "There were many Eskimos camped on the Kobuk River and one of their shamans determined to kill Dihch'i'ts'ik." After some adventures he dealt with this Eskimo shaman: "and within a year every Eskimo on the Kobuk had died. Dihch'i'ts'ik's medicine had been too strong for them." Dihch'i'ts'ik then died as an old man.

This story was probably learned from Sarah Shaaghan Dik (Old lady of the source) (G), the paternal grandmother of Johnny Frank and one of the foremost historians of the early life of the Nendaaghe and Too Loghe Hʉt'aane Koyukon and the Di'hąįį Gwich'in. She translated the Koyukon names into Di'hąįį Gwich'in very nicely. She survived three battles or ambushes and two husbands. Her first husband, Ch'igii Oonta' (He holds a child, he holds an unborn calf*),[†] was either a Nendaaghe Hʉt'aane Koyukon or Too Loghe Hʉt'aane Koyukon man and the second was Dits'ii K'iitł'uu, the Di'hąįį Gwich'in patriarch who came from K'iitł'uu[123] a community at the mouth of the Eł tsyeeh no'[124] (John River). She survived one battle while living among the Di'hąįį Gwich'in, and survived two battles as a member of the Nendaaghe and Too Loghe Hʉt'aane Koyukon nations. We know that she survived the last battle at Anaktuvuk Pass (K'iitł'it in Gwich'in) between one or more of the three bands

---

* The last translation is more correct for the traditional time period. This would mean that he was such a good provider that he was able to bring home an unborn calf for the elderly.

† Translated from the Koyukon original by Sarah Shaaghan Dik

of the Kuukpiġmiut Iñupiat of the Kuukpik (Colville River) and the
Nendaaghe and Too Loghe Hut'aane Koyukon. This story suggests
that she either visited the upper Kobuk River valley, lived in the
upper Kobuk River valley for a period of time, or someone else
within her generation did so. Sarah Shaaghan Dik was an old woman
when she died around the turn of the century. If she had been born
in 1817, give or take a few years, she could have lived in the upper
Noatak, Kobuk, and Alatna rivers and as a child be able to remember
events taking place during the 1820s and 1830s.

Basically the story says, (1) Dinilthoo and Dihch'i'ts'ik belonged
to two rival families and/or nations which were feuding, (2)
Dihch'i'ts'ik was of the Nendaaghe Hut'aane Koyukon nation, (3)
Dinilthoo was most likely a Saakił Hut'aane Koyukon, (4) the scene
is set in the Kobuk River valley; we may assume it is the upper
Kobuk River valley, (5) a number of Nendaaghe Hut'aane Koyukon
were living in the upper Kobuk valley, (6) a few members of the
Saakił Hut'aane Koyukon may have joined the Nendaaghe and Too
Loghe Hut'aane Koyukon in their eastward movement, (7) there is
persistent conflict with the central Kobuk Akuniġmiut Iñupiat, and
(8) there had to have been a major epidemic, warfare, or severe
famine in the Kobuk River valley for almost every "Eskimo" to
have died. The smallpox epidemic on the Yukon River of 1839 must
have had repercussions on the upper Kobuk because of the trade
contacts that went on every year between all Interior groups. Here
we have confirmation of conflict between two Koyukon nations,
the Saakił Hut'aane Koyukon and the Nendaaghe Hut'aane Koyukon.
The Nendaaghe Hut'aane Koyukon were also in persistent conflict
with the Akuniġmiut Iñupiat. This story must have occurred in the
same time frame as Pigliġiaq and Immałuuraq's story of Sayyen.
The period of conflict seems to have begun about 1820 and continued
shortly after 1840. These events would have set the stage for the
rapid assimilation of Iñupiat language and customs by the Saakił
Hut'aane Koyukon during the 1840s and, as Burch suggested,
definately between 1850 and 1880.

The Archaeological Record

The area of the central Brooks Range was once occupied in the Late Prehistoric period (circa A.D. 1250–1850) by people assumed to be Iñupiat. Later they were assumed to be Kutchin[125] (see below). Archaeological reports from Etivlik (Narvaŋuluk[126]), Tukuto, Kurupa, Chandler, Tulugaq, Galbraith, and Itkillik lakes suggest a continuum of artifacts for tool traditions through time, with the Late Prehistoric period being the last. Many of these sites, especially the numerous sites in the Itkillik Kuuŋa (or Ulu) and Atigun valleys, are not dated or there are so few artifacts (at some sites) that they cannot be assigned to a specific tool tradition. Tukuto Lake is situated to the west of the Itivliim (Etivluk River) near the head of Tukuto Creek and Etivlik (meaning "portage".[127]) Lake (Narvaŋuluk) is at the head of the Nigu River (Aalaasuuraq) to the southeast of Tukuto Lake. The Aalaasuuraq runs into the Itivliim Kuuŋa (Etivluk River) just above Tukuto Creek.

At Narvaŋuluk (Etivlik Lake) there was a fairly large community with forty houses thought to be contemporaneous and occupied approximately between post-1250 and 1700.[128] The late William N. Irving stated: "The geographic location of these [Narvaŋuluk] sites is of interest when it is considered that they lie near the source of three great river systems draining south, west and north, and that Itivik Lake [Narvaŋuluk] is well known as a way station on the pre-historic trade route between Kotzebue and Point Barrow."[129] The artifacts resembled those found along the Kobuk River for the same time period by archaeologist J. L. Giddings.[130] Giddings says of the Kobuk River assemblage: "Analysis of the 700 or more years of archaeology [from circa A.D. 1250] continuous from the present occupation of the river led to the definition of an "Arctic Woodland culture" as a continuity which is identical with neither the Eskimo or the Athapascan neighboring cultures, even thouth it incorporates elements of both."[131] Archaeological evidence from two sites at Tukuto Lake (Sikuruk and Croxton) suggests a fairly continuous occupation with a few brief interludes from the last 4420–3350 years before present.[132] In the general area between Howard Pass and the Aalaasuuraq (Nigu River) there are three lakes that deserve mentioning. They are Kinyiksukvik Lake (not named on USGS maps), which is right on the Howard Pass divide and Kipmik and Kikitaliorak lakes, which are about twenty miles to the southeast of Howard Pass and ten to fifteen miles to the southwest of Narvaŋuluk (Etivlik Lake). Each of these lakes has settlements of at least two to five houses often on the north and south shores. The Kipmik Lake site is thought to be Late Prehistoric; the other sites have not been dated.[133] The construction of the houses at those sites are unique in that they are partly constructed with sandstone slabs. In the Late Prehistoric times, within the last 250 years, a group or groups of people lived around the lakes at the headwaters of the Colville and Noatak rivers. The assumption has been that these groups were Iñupiat.

However, it is very difficult to tell the difference between Iñupiat, Koyukon, or Gwich'in sites along the Brooks Range[134] since the technologies in the region are similar. Also, even though there are comparative site-data for earlier periods, there are none for the Late Prehistoric time period specifically in the Brooks Range.[135] In regard to the sites at Tukuto Lake, archaeologists S. Craig Gerlach and Edwin S. Hall, Jr. stated that, "Thus, the earliest Late Prehistoric Eskimo occupation of the Tukuto Lake area may have been just after A.D. 1400 by a few people utilizing tents with slightly Semisubterranean floors and without interior hearths. This population probably infiltrated the Brooks Range from the south as artifact types from the Sikoruk site correspond closely with those from sites along the Noatak and Kobuk River drainages. Later in time, exploitation of the resources around the lake intensified. The majority of the houses constructed at the site-typically deep, Semisubterranean houses and 'half' houses—were inhabited between A.D. 1550 and 1750. This period of intense site use was followed by an historic occupation of a very few people living in tents with

Fig. 8. Looking south on Tukuto Lake. Photo by Charles Gil Mull.

Fig. 9. Looking southeast on Tukuto Lake. Photo by Charles Gil Mull.

Fig. 10. Looking north from Tukuto Lake. Photo by Charles Gil Mull.

Fig. 11. Looking south across Tukuto Lake. Photo by Charles Gil Mull.

Semisubterranean floor and interior hearths. The final pre-modern occupation may have been the result of specialized utilization of the site by hunters or trappers residing in ground-level tents for relatively short periods of time."[136] The late occupation date of 1750 at Tukuto Lake may be extended to 1850.[137] Furthermore, Gerlach in his notes questioned whether these sites weren't Athabascan Indian and not Iñupiat.

Kurupa Lake is situated to the northeast of Narvaŋuluk (Etivlik Lake) at the head of the Kurupa River, which is a north slope drainage. Kurupa Lake is the site of a major chert outcrop. Thousands of artifacts have been taken from the Kurupa Lake sites. Kenneth M. Shoenberg, an archaeologist for the National Parks Service in Alaska, conservatively remarked "In a more speculative vein, however, it seems probable that the people of the Kurupa phase [the period just before Late Prehistoric] followed a seasonal round that involved a summer and fall occupation on the northside of the Brooks Range, where the fall migration of caribou was intercepted. In the spring, they would have moved to the south side of the Brooks Range for an intercept of the spring migration of caribou moving north. A site such as the Toyuk site (Campbell;[138] Alexander 1969[139]), located on the south side of the Brooks Range and between the Hunt Fork and the John River, and with an assemblage containing a side-notched point, microblades and a burin would seem to represent such a pattern. In addition to Anderson (1972: 90[140]) suggests that "during several periods the region from the upper Noatak to Anaktuvuk Pass has formed a single culture area."[141] Most of the artifacts were from an earlier period. There were obsidian tools found which came from the Batza Tèna obsidian site on the middle Koyukuk River, with the exception of one piece whose source has not been traced.[142] This would suggest that at least one piece of obsidian might have been a trade item from Siberia. On a less speculative vein, Schoenberg says, "Numerous sites in the Kurupa region (such as KIR-155) indicate use of the area over the last several hundred years by late prehistoric and historic Eskimo groups."[143] Once again, the artifact inventory is such that one cannot distinguish Late Prehistoric Iñupiat from Athabascan, but it is enough that Kurupa Lake sites are a part of one continuous cultural area between the Noatak and Anaktuvuk Pass.

Douglas D. Anderson's paper on the archaeology of the Noatak drainage is particularly relevant. In his conclusions Anderson stated: "During some periods there seems also to have been a cultural separation between the lower and upper half of the Noatak drainage. Assemblages of the upper part (including the middle and upper zones) were closely affilitated with those from the Anaktuvuk Pass region and areas southeast of there, but unrelated to those nearer the Noatak river mouth or adjacent coast. The Kayuk-like assemblage represents one of these. It is interesting that cultural distinction between the western and eastern tundra areas has also been noted by Hall (1970)[144] for the late prehistoric times, and perhaps similar factors may prove to explain both cases."[145]

Batza Tèna needs special mention. Batza Tèna is situated between the Indian and Little Indian rivers on the east side of the Koyukuk River between the Kanuti and Hogatza rivers. It is an important site because the obsidian found and worked there has found its way all over the central Brooks Range.[146] One item that was found at Batza Tèna, however, was a jade (nephrite) adze (site Rkih-32) which originated on the Kobuk River.[147] According to Giddings the usage of nephrite was not common on the Kobuk until after 1400.[148] The upper Kobuk valley itself has been continuously occupied since 1000.[149] This serves to demonstrate the flow of at least one trade item between the Kobuk and Koyukuk rivers after 1400.

Taking the archaeological record from the present perspective, this would suggest that the area around Tukuto, Narvaŋuluk (Etivlik Lake), Kipmik, Kunyaksukvik, Kikialiorak, and Kurupa lakes and the area between the upper Noatak to Anaktuvuk Pass may have been occupied by Athabascan speaking people and not Iñupiat people during the Late Prehistoric times. Also the communities at Tukuto and Narvaŋuluk (Etivlik Lake) lakes were large communities, not

small family groups as described for the Too Loghe Hut'aane
Koyukon specifically. It is noteworthy that the settlement at
Narvaŋuluk (Etivlik Lake) was abandoned before the settlement at
Tukuto Lake. Taking all of the archaeological information at hand,
this means that the Nendaaghe and Too Loghe Hut'aane Koyukon
or Iyaġaaġmiut occupied Nendaaghe/Iyaġaaq between
approximately post 1250 and 1400 to 1850, a period of 450 to 600
years. My inclination is that the Koyukon first visited the area of the
upper Noatak from the Kobuk River in hunting parties and, as the
weather warmed, they moved into the area into permanent structures
circa 1400. This would verify the twentieth-century Iñupiat oral
tradition that the Iyaġaaġmiut were in the headwaters district of the
upper Noatak from the earliest times.

PART 1, CHAPTER NOTES

1. Ernest S. Burch, Jr., "Boundaries and Borders in Early contact North-Central Alaska," *Arctic Anthropology*, 35, no. 2 (1998a): 29.

2. Catherine Attla, personal communication, 1998.

3. Eliza Jones and Jules Jette, *Koyukon Athabascan Dictionary*, ms. (Fairbanks: Alaska Native Language Center, University of Alaska, 2000).

4. Annette McFayden-Clark, *Koyukuk River Culture*, National Museum of Man Mercury Series, Canadian Ethnology Service Paper No. 18 (1974): 83.

5. Sephard Krech, III, "On The Aboriginal Population Of The Kutchin," *Arctic Anthropology*, XV-1 (1978): 96.

6. Katherine Louise Arndt, "Dynamics of the Fur Trade of the Middle Yukon River, Alaska, 1839–1868," (thesis, Fairbanks, Alaska, 1996): Appendix 1, pg. 204.

7. Isabell Charlie, personal communication, November 1998.

8. Peter John, interview by James M. Kari, 3 February 1999.

9. Robert McKennan, "Anent The Kutchin Tribes," *American Anthropology*, 37 no. 2, (1933): 369.

10. Frederick Hadleigh-West, "On the Distribution and Territories of Western Kutchin Tribes," *Anthropology Papers of the University of Alaska* 7, no. 2 (1959): 114.

11. Ernest S. Burch, Jr., *Iñupiaq Eskimo Nations of Northwest Alaska*, (Fairbanks: University of Alaska Press, 1998b).

12. Ernest S. Burch, Jr., and Craig W. Mishler, "The Di'hąįį Gwich'in: Mystery People of Northern Alaska," *Arctic Anthropology* 32, no. 1 (1995): 147–172.

13. Ibid. (1998b): 8.

14. Ibid.

15. Ibid. (1998a): 26.

16. Ibid.: 9–10.

17. Ibid.: 5.

18. Arndt (1996:) 7, "The section of the river between Fort Yukon and Nulato is here designated the Middle Yukon."

19. Michael E. Krauss, map of "Native Peoples and Languages of Alaska," (Fairbanks: Alaska Native Language Center, revised 1982).

20. Annette McFadyen-Clark, "Koyukon," *Handbook of North American Indians, Subarctic* 6, ed. June Helms, (1981): 582.

21. Jones and Jette, *Koyukon Athabascan Dictionary*, ms.

22. Margaret Matthews, et.al., "Stevens Village Land Use Plan, Ethnogeography of Ancestral Lands and Integrated Resources Management Plan," (Stevens Village, Alaska: Stevens Village Council, 1999): 65.

23. Frederick Whymper, *Travel and Adventure in the Territory of Alaska*, 2nd ed. (Readex Microprint Corporation, 1966): 182.

24. Ibid., 210.

25. William H. Dall, *Alaska and Its Resources*, 2nd ed. (Arno & The New York Times, 1970): 428.

26. Church Missionary Record, vol. 2, n.s. (December 1872): 396.

27. Ibid., (1872): 397.

28. Frederica de Laguna, *The Prehistory of Northern North America as Seen From the Yukon*, The Society For American Archaeology, no. 3, Of Memoirs of the Society (Menasha, Wisconsin, 1947): 39.

29. L. A. Zagoskin, *Lieutenant Zagoskin's Travels In Russian America 1842–1844: The First Ethnographic and Geographic Investigations in the Yukon and Kuskokwim Valley of Alaska*, ed. Henry N. Michael, (Toronto: University of Toronto Press, 1967): 146. "The word for "river" in the coastal speech of the Chnagmyut."

30. Ibid., 144, 166, 177, 178, 180, "All of this plain along the river, from the Nulato parallel down river as far as Khogoltlinde, is occupied by Takayaksa native, who are relatives of the Ulukagmyut. In translation *takayaksa* means "swamp."

31. Lawrence Kaplan, personal communication, 1999.

32. Burch, personal communication, 1998.

33. Zagoskin (1967):143.

34. Ibid., 152.

35. Jones and Jette, *Koyukon Athabascan Dictionary*, ms.

36. Zagoskin (1967): 153.

37. Eliza Jones, personal communication with present orthography, 1998.

38. Zagoskin, (1967): 153.

39. Eliza Jones and Catherine Attla, personal communication, 1998.

40. The editor Henry N. Michael asserts this is the Selawik River.

41. Zagoskin, (1967): 153.

42. de Laguna (1947): 29.

43. Eliza Jones, personal communication, 1999.

44. Ibid.

45. Ibid.

46. Jules Jette, ms., (1910).

47. James M. Kari, personal communication, 1999.

48. Donald W. Clark, personal communication, 30 January 1998.

49. Eliza Jones, personal communication, November 1998).

50. Burch and Mishler (1995): 153.

51. Donald W. Clark, personal communication, 1998.

52. Moses Henzie, *Moses Henzie*, Yukon-Koyukuk School District Series, (Vancouver, B. C.: Hancock House Publishers Ltd., 1979): 14.

53. Henry Bekk'oyoodaałdleede, *Chief Henry Yugh Nollonigee: The Stories of Chief Henry*, transl. and transc. Eliza Jones (Fairbanks: Alaska Native Language Center, 1979): 62; Bekk'oyoodaałdleede means "his arrow doesn't miss," Eliza Jones, personal communication, 1999.

54. Donald W. Clark, personal communication, January 1998.

55. Leonard John, "How Stevens Village Came To Be," *Alaska Sportsman*, (September 1959): 32.

56. James Taylor White, notebook, n.d. (Fairbanks: University of Alaska Fairbanks Archives, Box 4, 21 March).

57. Matthews et.al., (1999): 54.

58. James M. Kari, personal communication, 1999.

59. Catherine Attla, personal communication, 1998.

60. W. L. Hardisty, Hudson Bay Company Archives, 1853; Robert McDonald, journal from 1862–1910:1867; W. H. Dall (1870, 1970): 431, Robert McKennan, field notes, University of Alaska Archives; Catherine McClellan, *Handbook of North American Indians*, ed. June Helm (1981): 37; Katherine Arndt (1996): 134; Richard I. Ruggles, *A Country So Interesting* (1991):57; A. P. Raboff, "Preliminary Study Of The Western Gwich'in," *American Indian Culture and Research Journal* 23, no. 2 (1999): 1–25.

61. Burch (1998a): 36.

62. Peter John, interview by James Kari, 3 February 1999.

63. Church Missionary Record 2, n.s. (December 1872): 396.

64. Burch (1998a): 29.

65. *Upper Koyukuk River Place Names* (Fairbanks: Alaska Native Language Center Library, University of Alaska Fairbanks, n.d.).

66. Moses Johnson, et. al., *"Allakaket-Alatna Area Native Placenames,"* comp. Eliza Jones with contributions by Wendy Arundale, ms., October 1997: 23.

67. Zagoskin (1967): 153.

68. Ibid.: 166 (This is probably the present-day Beaver Creek, editors, A.I.N.A.)

69. Jones and Jette, ms.

70. Catherine Attla, personal communication, 1998.

71. Sydney Huntington and Jim Reardon, *Shadows on the Koyukuk* (Portland: Alaska Northwest Books, 1998): 132.

72. Burch (1998a): 34.

73. J. L. Giddings, *"Dendrochronology in Northern Alaska,"* University of Alaska publication IV (1942): 63.

74. Huntington (1998): 132.

75. Zagoskin (1967): 152.

76. Annette McFadyen Clark, *Who Lived in This House? A Study of Koyukuk River Semisubterranean Houses*, Mercury Series, Archaeological Survey of Canada, Paper 153 (Quebec: Canadian Museum of Civilization, 1998): 31.

77. James W. Van Stone and Ives Goddard, "Territorial Groups of West-Central Alaska Before 1898," *Handbook of North American Indians* 6, ed. June Helms (Washington, D. C.: Smithsonian Institute, 1981): 557.

78. Rochfort Maguire, *The Journal of Rochfort Maguire 1853–1854*, ed. John Bockstoce (London: The Hakluyt Society, 1988): 43.

79. Ibid.: 502.

80. Edwin S. Hall, Jr., "The Late Prehistoric/Early Historic Eskimos of Interior Northern Alaska: An Ethnoarcheological Approach?" *Anthropological Papers of the University of Alaska* 15, no. 1 (1970): 2. "...who lived along the upper Colville above the mouth of the Killik and along its tributaries and at times moved into the Noatak drainage."

81. Ernest S. Burch, Jr., *The Cultural and Natural Heritage of Northwest Alaska, Vol. VII* (Kotzebue, Alaska: International Affairs, NANA Museum of the Arctic and Anchorage, Alaska: The U. S. National Parks Service, 1998c): 7.

82. Maguire (1988): 543.

83. Maguire (1988): 367.

84. John Murdoch, "Ethnological results of the Point Barrow Expedition," *9th Annual Report of the Bureau of American Ethnology for Years 1887–1888*, (Washington, D. C., 1892): 19–441.

85. Alexander Hunter Murray, *Journal of the Yukon 1847–48*, (Ottowa: Government Printing Bureau, 1910): 11.

86. Murray (1910): 57.

87. Burch (1998b): 245. Burch covers this nation in Chapter 11.

88. John C. Cantwell, "A Narrative of the Exploration of the Kowak River, Alaska," *Report of the Cruise of the Revenue Marine Steamer Corwin in the Arctic Ocean* (Washington, D. C.: U. S. Revenue Cutter Service, 1885).

89. George M. Stoney, *Exploration in Alaska*, 2nd ed. (Seattle: The Shorey Book Store, 1900): 828. First published in the U. S. Naval Institute Proceedings of September and December 1899.

90. Burch (1998b): 135.

91. Burch, et. al. (1998): 11.

92. Burch (1998b): 135

93. Huntington (1998): 132.

94. Burch (1998a): 25.

95. Ibid.: 28.

96. Douglas Anderson, Wanni W. Anderson, Ray Bane, Richard K. Nelson, Nita Sheldon Towarak, *Kuuvaŋmiut Subsistence: Traditional Eskimo Life in the Latter Twentieth Century*, 2nd ed. (Northwest Arctic Borough School District, 1992): 105.

97. Burch (1998a): 28.

98. Eliza Jones, personal communication, 1999.

99. Loreena Williams, personal communication, 1999.

100. Hannah Mendenhall, Ruthie Sampson and Edward Tennant, eds., *Lore of the Iñupiat, Vol. 1*, (Kotzebue, Alaska: Northwest Arctic Borough School District, 1992): 30.

101. Sun, *My Life and Other Stories*, comp. David Libbey (Kotzebue, Alaska: NANA Museum of the Arctic, 1985): 6. Also Qalamiut.

102. Ibid., map at beginning of book.

103. Linda Piquk Lee, Ruthie Tatqaviñ Sampson and Edward Tennant, eds., *Lore of the Iñupiat, Vol. 3* (Alaska: Northwest Arctic Borough School District, 1992): 15, 21.

104. Sun (1985): 6, 7.

105. Nicholas J. Gubser, *"Comparative Study of the Intellectual Culture of the Nunamiut Eskimos at Anaktuvuk Pass, Alaska,"* (Fairbanks: University of Alaska, 1961): 92.

106. Sun (1985): 5.

107. J. L. Giddings, *Kobuk River People*, Studies of Northern Peoples Number 1, (Fairbanks: University of Alaska Fairbanks: Department of Anthropology, 1961): 99–103.

108. Burch (1998b): 111.

109. Ibid. : 344.

110. Loreena Williams, personal communication, 1999.

111. Sun (1985): 114.

112. Giddings (1961): 100.

113. Sun (1985): 115.

114. Giddings (1961): 105.

115. Ruthie Sampson, personal communication, 1999.

116. Levi Mills, Burch field notes, Kotzebue, Alaska, 18 February 1986.

117. Dikajaw, also Dik-a-chók, Allakaket Church Records, 28 July 1924).

118. Bertha Moses, personal communication, 1998.

119. Ibid.

120. Sun (1985): 77–79

121. Robert Nasruk Cleveland, Burch, field notes, 30 January 1970; Bertha Nictune Moses, Raboff notes, 1998.

122. Robert McKennan, *The Chandalar Kutchin*, Arctic Institute of North America Technical Paper No. 17 (New York, 1965): 81.

123. Steven Tsee Gho', Tsyaa Tsal Peter, Sr., personal communication, 1987–97. This reference will be shortened to STP, 1987–97 throughout this text.

124. *Upper Koyukuk River Place Names,* no. 57 (Fairbanks: Alaska Native Language Center Library, University of Alaska Fairbanks, n.d.): 138.

125. Kenneth M. Schoenberg, *The Archaeology of Kurupa Lake* (Anchorage: United States Department of the Interior, National Parks Service, 1985): 143, table 9.

126. Burch (1998b): 116.

127. William N. Irving, *Preliminary Report of an Archaeological Reconnaissance in the Western part of the Brooks Range of Alaska* (Cambridge: Peabody Museum, Harvard University, 1954): 6.

128. Ibid.: 8, 9.

129. Ibid.

130. J. L. Giddings, "Alaska Aboriginal Culture," *National Survey of Historic Sites and Buildings, Theme XVI, Indigenous Peoples and Cultures* (Anchorage: National Parks Service, Anchorage Area Office, 1962): 91.

131. Ibid.: 91.

132. S. Craig Gerlach and Edwin S. Hall, Jr., "The Later Prehistory of Northern Alaska: The View from Tukuto Lake," A*laska Anthropological Association Monograph Series #4*, (Fairbanks: University of Alaska, 1988): 118.

133. Robert Gal, personal communication, November, 1999.

134. John P. Cook, personal communication, 1998.

135. Douglas D. Anderson, personal communication, 1999.

136. Hall and Gerlach (1988): 117.

137. S. Craig Gerlach, personal communication, 1999.

138. John M. Campbell, "Cultural Succession at Anaktuvuk Pass, Arctic Alaska," *Prehistoric Cultural Relations Between the Arctic and Temperate Zones of North America*, ed. John Campbell, Arctic Institute of North America, Technical Paper No. 11 (1969): 39–54.

139. Herbert Alexander, "Prehistory of the Central Brooks Range-An Archaeological Analysis," (Ph.D. diss., University of Oregon, University Microfilms, Ann Arbor, 1969).

140. Douglas D. Anderson, "An Archaeological Survey of Noatak Drainage, Alaska" *Arctic Anthropology* 9(1) (1972): 66–102.

141. Schoenberg (1985): 144.

142. Kenneth Schoenberg, personal communication, October 1999.

143. Schoenberg (1985): 149.

144. Hall (1970).

145. Anderson (1972): 100.

146. Donald W. Clark and A. McFadyen Clark, "Batza Tèna, Trail of Obsidian, Archaeology at an Alaska Obsidian Source," *Archaeological Survey of Canada Mercury Series Paper 147* (Canadian Museum of Civilization, 1993).

147. Ibid.: 187.

148. J. L. Giddings, "The Denbigh Flint Complex," *American Antiquity* 16, no. 3 (1951): 193–202.

149. Anderson, et. al. (1992): 22.

PART II

THE PANNIAQ ACCOUNTS

THE PANNIAQ ACCOUNTS

We have one more authority on the history of the early Iñupiat and Koyukon relaationships in the Kobuk and Noatak rivers—the late Simon Panniaq Paneak (born 1900) of Anaktuvuk Pass, Alaska (Fig.12). Panniaq painted a very large picture:

> I was talking about old Indians who was raised over at head Noatak and Kobuk, just between there, nearby,…we don't know or nobody talking about how many years those Indians staying over in that area. This is a very, very long time ago but later on, somehow there was a mix up between Kobuk and the Indian because the Indians was jealous about the hunting grounds and Kobuk people can't stand without it too, because they want to hunt too,…and then there was kind of quarreling and they became enemies of each other.
>
> Finally they started to fight, killed one another and finally they began a big fighting and one at a time and then from generation to generation, they said **that one time they almost kill all the Kobuk one group almost.*** Indians, there are too many in those [days] too I believe— almost they kill them all off, [...The Kobuk people had fences built around their community, but the Indians tore them down†] And then one boy he jumped off the fence

---

* Emphasis by APR.
† Edited by APR.

Fig. 12. Simon Panniaq Paneak. Courtesy of Dr. Robert Rauch.

[Sikirgaurak[1]] and he run away to get to another people from down below [Akuniġmiut Iñupiat] and a bunch of Kobuk people going up to where the Indians are...they fought them off—Indians can't hardly stand it any longer and they beat it.

...I guess that not many men left; they didn't want to stay where they used to live in that area and over in upper Kobuk and Noatak in the mountain there and they called them Uyaġaaġmiut [a dialect variant[*]] in these very old days, they love to stay in the rocks, they don't have an axe...that's why they like to stay in the rocks during the summer time, Eskimo also like to make a stone house too, according to story they were telling,...And Indians [Uyaġaaġmiut] moving from there to the northern Brooks Range near Howard Pass, over there where the Eskimo and Nunamiut were too and stayed over there for a long time and same thing when the Indians [Uyaġaaġmiut grow up they became an unfriendly people and jealous (of) the ground.

---

* Levi Mills. Uyaġaaq was the name for the Noatak-Alatna headwaters. Uyaġaaġmiut, then, were people from that area. Burch notes, Kotzebue, Alaska, February 18, 1986.

> And Eskimo don't like it that way, they could kill all
> the animals, as much as they could catch but Indians
> [Uyaġaaġmiut] (didn't)—...they love to take a limit
> because sounds like to me they are smart people they don't
> want to kill all the animals...[where] ever they used to
> live, they thought it might be, they might have animals for
> next year, for future...[2]

Upon examination, Panniaq establishes (1) the Nendaaghe
Hut'aane Koyukon (Uyaġaaġmiut,* Uyaġaaġmiit, and Iyaġaaġmiit
are all dialect variants[3]) firmly at the headwaters of the Nunataaq
(Noatak River) and upper Kobuk River at the earliest times before
Iñupiat incursion; (2) he also points out the obvious—territoriality
was predicated on hunting rights to a given area; (3) the absolute
dependence of the Akuniġmiut Iñupiat and Saakił Hut'aane Koyukon
on the fall caribou and sheep hunt in the upper Nunataaq (Noatak);
(4) the gradual increase in hostilities; (5) prolonged conflict over
several generations (generally a series of twenty-year periods) which
could mean a period of sixty years; (6) one band of the Saakił
Hut'aane Koyukon was almost wiped out by the Nendaaghe Hut'aane
Koyukon; (7) 'Saakił Hut'aane Koyukon appealed to their downriver
Akuniġmiut Iñupiat relatives and neighbors, whom we might point
out shared in the fall caribou and sheep hunt in the upper Nunataaq
(Noatak); (8) a devastating defeat for the Nendaaghe Hut'aane
Koyukon in the upper Kobuk; (9) withdrawal northward of the
Nendaaghe Hut'aane Koyukon closer to their northern Iñupiat
neighbors the Kuukpiġmiut (Qaŋmaliġmiut, Killiġmiut, and
Kaŋianiġmiut bands); and (10) the hostilities were resumed along
the Nendaaghe Hut'aane Koyukon northern boundaries. Panniaq has
presented one of the fullest pictures of the Uyaġaaġmiut, the
Nendaaghe and Too Loghe Hut'aane Koyukon and, as we shall see,
their subsequent activities as well.

---

* I will use Uyaġaaġmiut throughout the remainder of this text, APR.

The idea of the Nendaaghe Hut'aane Koyukon moving to the headwaters of the Alaasuuraq (Nigu River) and Howard Pass[4] are as stated first by Panniaq, reported by Gubser, and later repeated by Hall[5] has been called into question by Burch and Mishler. They argue that the Howard Pass area is uninhabitable during the winter and that it is more likely that the Uyaġaaġmiut simply withdrew to the headwaters of the Nunataaq (Noatak River) valley.[6] The Nendaaghe Hut'aane Koyukon may not have lived in the Howard Pass area during the winter, but since it was within their original estate, they at least frequented the area during the summer months as Panniaq suggested. Here we need to take into account the two Late Prehistoric settlements at Kipmik Lake and, although it is not certain, the Kikitaliorak Lake site about twenty miles to the east of Howard Pass and to the southwest of Narvaŋuluk (Etivlik Lake) and the settlements at Kinyiksukvik Lake in Howard Pass. The houses at Kipmik and Kikitaliorak sites were constructed partly with sandstone slabs, thereby differing significantly in construction from those of other locations.[7] Kipmik Lake is located between the upper Nunataaq (Noatak) and Narvaŋuluk (Etivlik Lake). The Koyukon were living in the upper Aalaasuk (Alatna River) valley during this interval, while the Kaŋianiġmiut regional band of the Kuukpiġmiut lived just below Itilyiargiok Creek (Itgiliagiaq, "the way to the Indians") along the Alaasuuraq (Nigu River).[8] If that was so, then by the late 1830s and early 1840s the Kaŋianiġmiut band was taking possession of northern Nendaaghe and pushing southward. Panniaq was explicit about this, "A long time ago Indians and Iñupiat were living at the head of the Colville River. The Indians having fled over from the Kobuk River. Having lived together for a while they finally began to fight again."[9] This would suggest that the Nendaaghe Hut'aane Koyukon were in the Howard Pass area and the upper Nunataaq (Noatak) and that the Too Loghe Hut'aane Koyukon were in the Aalaasuk (Alatna River) valley, each in their own estate. The overriding point here is that the Nendaaghe Hut'aane Koyukon shifted from one area within their own estate to another.

Many of the Iñupiat/Koyukon conflicts between the Nunataaq (Noatak) and Kobuk rivers attributed to the Saakił Hut'aane Koyukon of the upper Kobuk were probably carried out by the Nendaaghe Hut'aane Koyukon during this time period. Burch, in *The Cultural and Natural Heritage of Northwest Alaska*, described a series of raids between the Kobuk Koyukon and Nuataaġmiut Iñupiat of the central Nunataaq (Noatak River) in detail.[10] That the Nendaaghe Hut'aane Koyukon would fight, for their estate, even in exile, certainly was to be expected.

In reviewing the upper Kobuk River prehistory we find that in the earliest time period it was occupied at its headwaters by the Saakił Hut'aane Koyukon who were know as Qalamui or Qalamiut by their Iñupiat neighbors, and in the central region it was occupied by the Akuniġmiut Iñupiat, the central Kobuk Iñupiat. The Nendaaghe Hut'aane Koyukon were a mountain people who lived at the headwaters of the Noatak, Alatna, and Colville rivers. Their estate was known as Uyaġaaq or Iyaġaaq and the residents of the area were known as Uyaġaaġmiut and Iyaġaaġmiut by the Iñupiat. They were also known as Nendaaghe Hut'aane Koyukon and their estate was known as Nendaaghe by the Koyukon. Archaeological evidence suggests that they had occupied the area for at least the previous 450 to 600 years up to about 1850. They lived at Nendaaghe year round. Each nations' borders and boundaries were clearly defined. All three groups were closely intermarried and interrelated. The Saakił Hut'aane Koyukon and Akuniġmiut Iñupiat men were in the habit of hunting for caribou and sheep in the fall time in the upper Nunataaq (Noatak) and sometimes ventured further north. Something happened during the early nineteenth century, perhaps colder weather, a caribou crash, famine, warfare, or a combination of those events, which forced some members of the Nendaaghe Hut'aane Koyukon to seek shelter with their Kobuk River relatives and/or trading partners. Ronald O. Skoog, in his dissertation of 1968, suggested that there was a caribou shortage sometime between 1840–1880.[11] His information, however, came from reports along the coast.

The shortage may have actually began ten or fifteen years earlier (1825–1830). It seems highly probable that the famine in the middle Koyukuk River extended throughout northwestern Interior Alaska. Also there is no way to determine the extent of the smallpox epidemic in the upper Koyukuk or Kobuk rivers during the 1839 outbreak that swept the lower Yukon River. Certainly the Koyukon trade routes went up the Koyukuk River and down the Kobuk River. As we shall see, there were at least two major defeats in warfare which left the women and children destitute, forcing them to seek food and shelter with their nearest relatives. In either case this suggests a fluid bilingualism among all three groups, at least among the men. After a number of years the Nendaaghe Hʉt'aane Koyukon returned to their former territory, but in the interim they returned on a seasonal basis for the hunt and left before winter set in. Once re-established in the upper Nunataaq (Noatak) and Howard Pass area, they decided to limit the take of their southern neighbors and relatives. Perhaps the caribou herd was still relatively small. This led to conflict which escalated into ambush and finally into open warfare. Sometime in the late 1830s or early 1840s the Nendaaghe Hʉt'aane Koyukon were defeated in the upper Kobuk. This brought about the rapid social and linguistic change of the Saakił Hʉt'aane Koyukon from Koyukon to Iñupiat within one generation. By the time of Stoney and Cantwell's visits in 1885–86 only the old men spoke Koyukon, and by the early twentieth century this transition was all but forgotten. The Nendaaghe Hʉt'aane Koyukon suffered a devastating defeat in the upper Kobuk, and no longer having the manpower available to defend their former territory, withdrew to the northern and eastern part of their estate within the next few years. As we shall see western Nendaaghe/Uyaġaaq (upper Noatak) was completely abandoned by the Nendaaghe Hʉt'aane Koyukon by 1845.

Nendaaghe the Northern Boundaries

Now for the upper Nunataaq (Noatak) and the northern boundaries. Burch called the upper Noatak, "The Headwaters

District," which he described as including "the Noatak River headwaters, the middle and upper sections of the Nigu River (Aalaasuuraq) valley, the Alatna River (Aalaasuk) headwaters, and the nearby slopes of the Schwatka and Endicott Mountains,"[12] in short, the western estate of Nendaaghe. The Noatak headwaters, he defined as, "an 80-mile (130-km) stretch of the Noatak valley between Ataongarak Creek and the Noatak River's source on the slopes of Mt. Igikpuk."[13] Immediately below this region, the Noatak River is occupied by the Nuataaġmiut Iñupiaq[14] (central Noatak). In the headwaters district however, Burch says, "the earliest occupants known to us via oral history were not Iñupiat, but Di'hại̦ Gwich'in, a nation of Athabaskan-speaking Indians. They were known to the Iñupiat as Uyaġaaġmiut,..."[15] As noted earlier Kobuk River people in general called the Nendaaghe and Too Loghe Hʉt'aane Koyukon, Iyaġaaġmiut, whereas the Anaktuvuk Pass people called them Uyaġaaġmiut. Burch goes on to say, "By the beginning of the nineteenth century they were already there. Their territory at the time seems to have encompassed the entire Endicott Mountain range, and thus extended a considerable distance east of the area of concern here. For at least a few years between 1810 and 1830, it also extended down the Nigu to the lower Etivluk River (Itivliim Kuuŋa) and adjacent sections of the upper Colville (Kaŋianiq)."[16] Here we have the estate of the Nendaaghe Hʉt'aane Koyukon, Nendaaghe/Uyaġaaq. The northwestern border and boundary we will accept at Ataongarak Creek along the upper Nunataaq (Noatak River) and along the Kuukpik (Colville) and Aalaasuk (Alatna River) rivers as outlined by Burch and his Iñupiat informants. Western Nendaaghe/Uyaġaaq was situated along a major east/west trade route which connected the Colville, Noatak, and Kobuk river and the Iñupiat from Bering Straits to those along the Arctic Ocean. This situation along a major trade route in the midst of Iñupiat neighbors must have triggered antagonism. But, before we can continue with Nendaaghe Hʉt'aane Koyukon estate and range in the north, I must address the issue of the Di'hại̦ Gwich'in presence in the upper

Nunataaq (Noatak) verus information that speaks very solidly for
the Nendaaghe and Too Loghe Hut'aane Koyukon presence in the
upper Noatak, Alatna, Colville, and John rivers.

Iyaġaaġmiut, Uyaġaaġmiut, and Di'hąįį Gwich'in

I think that Burch,[17] Burch and Mishler,[18] and Burch[19] were
following the lead of Hall,[20] Hall,[21] Gubser,[22] Ingstad,[23] and Panniaq
in assuming that the Nendaaghe and Too Loghe Hut'aane Koyukon
were the Di'hąįį Gwich'in. I agree with Hall, Burch, and Burch and
Mishler, Gubser, Ingstad, and their informants that there was an
Athabascan-speaking people in the headwaters district; however, I
do not agree that they were Di'hąįį Gwich'in. They were, in fact,
Nendaaghe Hut'aane Koyukon, the Uyaġaaġmiut who were in
Nendaaghe/ Uyaġaaq initially. One of the major points that has
brought about confusion is the fact that the combined Nendaaghe
and Too Loghe Hut'aane Koyukon eastward displacement took place
in stages (at least between 1820–1867) and for a period of twenty
years (1845–1867) or more the Nendaaghe and Too Loghe Hut'aane
Koyukon were living in the upper Chandalar River and specifically
at Chehłee Van[24] (Chandalar Lake) on the Di'hąįį estate.[25]
Consequently a whole generation of Iñupiat (most of the Iñupiaq
informants) would have assumed that the group names of
Uyaġaaġmiut, Uyaġaaġmiit, Iyaġaaġmiit, and Iyaġaaġmiut lived only
in the Chandalar River area. Also, during the famine that ended in
the 1840s and the caribou crash of the 1880s in northwestern Alaska,
many people were dislocated and moved elsewhere with group
information or died. Furthermore, it was during the 1920s when the
Nunamiut* were visiting Fort Yukon, Alaska, that a chance meeting
with a survivor of the Anaktuvuk Pass attack was met[26] and it was
that meeting which solidified the notion that Gwich'in people were
the Uyaġaaġmiut. If it were not for Pigliġiaq, Immałuuraq, Dikajaw,
Panniaq, Sarah Shaaghan Dik, Johnny Frank, Steven Tsee Gho' Tsyaa

---

* Present name of Anaktuvuk Pass residents.

Tsal Peter, Sr., and others, we would not know that the Nendaaghe and Too Loghe Hʉt'aane Koyukon originally lived in the upper Noatak, upper Alatna, the Nigu, the lower Etivluk, or John rivers. It was not Di'hąįį Gwich'in who lived there. It was the Nendaaghe and Too Loghe Hʉt'aane Koyukon who lived in this area—known as Nendaaghe by the Koyukon and Uyaġaaq by the Iñupiat—and became refugees, joining the Di'hąįį Gwich'in after 1845 and continuing to live on the Di'hąįį estate after the eastward displacement of the Di'hąįį Gwich'in. In fact, I believe that the Nendaaghe and Too Loghe Hʉt'aane Koyukon transition from the Nendaaghe/ Uyaġaaq estate to Chehłee Van (Chandalar Lake) took place in one generation, between 1845 and 1847.

There is no doubt in my mind that the Nendaaghe and Too Loghe Hʉt'aane Koyukon and the Di'hąįį Gwich'in were closely allied as neighbors. The Di'hąįį Gwich'in called the remaining Nendaaghe and Too Loghe Hʉt'aane Koyukon, K'iitł'it Gwich'in. The K'iitł'it Gwich'in spoke Koyukon and the Di'hąįį Gwich'in spoke Dinjii Zhuh.*[27] I would suggest that they engaged each other in trade with formal trading partnerships and, in war, held joint seasonal caribou drives, intermarried, held feasts with the each other, shared many beliefs or were at least cognizant of the others' belief systems, helped each other out in war, and traveled through each others' range on a seasonal basis. There was a fair amount of bilingualism among the three groups and from time to time members of one nation became the members of the other nation. We know that members of the Nendaaghe and Too Loghe Hʉt'aane Koyukon joined the Di'hąįį Gwich'in after the K'iitł'it/Anaktuvuk Pass battle as evidenced by Sarah Shaaghan Dik and others. I am positive this was not an isolated incident. The Nendaaghe and Too Loghe Hʉt'aane Koyukon also appealed to the Di'hąįį Gwich'in for assistance much as the Saakił Hʉt'aane Koyukon appealed to their neighbors, the Akuniġmiut Iñupiat. In the case of the Di'hąįį Gwich'in, we know that they hired

* Dinjii Zhuh Ginjik. Currently known as the Gwich'in language.

themselves out as mercenaries; perhaps the same held true for the Akuniġmiut Iñupiat. The degree of interaction, cooperation, or hostilities between the Nendaaghe and Too Loghe Hut'aane Koyukon and the Di'hạịị Gwich'in all depended on circumstances.

A prime example of a person going from Nendaaghe Hut'aane Koyukon territory to the Di'hạịị Gwich'in for assistance is Kọ̀'ehdan (Without fire coals) (G) who appealed to the Di'hạịị Gwich'in for shelter and aide. They helped him in a retaliatory offensive. One of the oldest Neets'ạịị Gwich'in stories about Iñupiat wars is the story of Kọ̀'ehdan. It was written by Richard Slobodin after a 1947 telling by William Ittza of Fort McPherson, N. W. T., Canada.[28] This version was told by Henry T'ạạval[29] Williams[30] and embellished by the late Steven Tsee Gho' Tsyaa Tsal Peter, Sr. T'ạạval and Tsee Gho' were cousins and learned the story through their grandmother and mothers respectively:

> It was springtime and Kọ̀'ehdan and his younger brother were having a feast for the men in the men's house. It was hot, so they took off their outer garments. When the Iñupiat came upon them, Kọ̀'ehdan and his brother slipped into their snowshoes and made a run for it. His brother was killed and so were all the men in the men's house. Kọ̀'ehdan escaped to safety on a steep cliff. One Iñupiaq named 'Khii Choo' (Big Silver/fall chum Salmon in Gwich'in, in Iñupiat that would be Iqaluġruaqpak[31]) was killing Kọ̀'ehdan's brother with a club. As he was doing so he said, " Kọ̀'ehdan, is that really you, is this your younger brother that I am doing this to?" Kọ̀'ehdan looked down upon the scene. He was helpless. He had no clothes and no weapon.
>
> The Iñupiat warriors finally marched off. Among them was his wife Łihteerạhdyaa (One whom we take back and forth). He asked her to mark her trail; she did this. Finally the last man was his trading partner. The man pleaded with him, "Kọ̀'ehdan come down to me." But Kọ̀'ehdan refused to come down to him, so his trading partner left him a pair of gloves.

He went back to the village to find his younger brother's wife wounded. They snared rabbits. They ate them and made a rabbit skin wrap for Kǫ'ehdan. She asked him to leave her since she was badly wounded. She had four dogs and they stayed with her. He took some coals with him to light his fires and set out to find people. The fire coals went out and for some time, until he found people, he had no fire, and he suffered greatly from the cold. That is why he is called Kǫ'ehdan, "Without fire coals." After a few days his sister-in-law's four dogs came after him, then he knew she had died.

He walked for many days and nights. He began to suffer greatly from hypothermia. He finally stumbled upon an old trail and followed that until he came to a new trail. He followed the new trail until he came upon a settlement.

He sneaked into the settlement and stumbled into the home of an elderly woman. He told her all that had happened and asked her not to reveal him right away. She fed him for a number of days, but a small boy who came to give her food inadvertantly saw her put the food aside (as if for someone else). The little boy immediately told all that he saw. Then the community was in a state of alert, they were ready for a fight, all the men gathered. The elderly lady ran out and cried, "My grandson, Kǫ'ehdan, sneaked into camp, but I did not tell about him."

Kǫ'ehdan revealed himself and immediately began to put together a group of warriors to take his revenge. He spent the summer recuperating and the community made preparations for the coming battle.

Then they started off in late August or early September during the fall chum salmon run. They went back to Kǫ'ehdan's former settlement and followed the trail of the aggressors. It was the better part of a month that they followed their trail, and finally they ended up along the shores of a big lake along the ocean shore.

His wife and the other women saw them and secretly

brought them food. Then under cover of the fog they cut up all the *umiaks*. They killed the Iñupiat there and took back their women. Kò'ehdan's wife slit the throat of her Iñupiat abductor. Meanwhile Kò'ehdan had warned his trading partner, and he was relieved to find that his trading partner was not among the dead men. He saw his trading partner at a distance then and asked him to come with them, but his trading partner replied, "You were the one whom I could not convince to come down to me, so now I must refuse you." Kò'ehdan left some food and those things that his trading partner would need to survive. They sang the "Divee ch'illig" (sheep song) and did a victory dance, then departed. That's how Kò'ehdan got his revenge.

The story basically says: (1) this was a continuation of hostilities between the Iñupiat and Nendaaghe Hʉt'aane Koyukon. Perhaps the presence of the Russians and Americans[32] in Hotham Inlet exacerbated the already festering situation; (2) the Nendaaghe Hʉt'aane Koyukon had a men's house, which is a different custom from the Neets'ạįį Gwich'in and the people of Kodeel Kkaakk'et village on the lower Koyukuk River who did not use the men's house *(qarġi)*, but made one for their visiting Iñupiat trading partners;[33] (3) Kò'ehdan and his Iñupiaq trading partner knew each other well and were able to offer each other protection; (4) as before, the Iñupiat and Nendaaghe Hʉt'aane Koyukon were able to communicate with each other fluently; (5) the Iñupiat raid took place during the spring when the snow was still on the ground, the Iñupiat also attacked in the spring at K'iitł'it/Anaktuvuk Pass; (6) Kò'ehdan's wife and other women were carried away by the Iñupiat; (7) Kò'ehdan went towards the general direction of another community which was quite away from his settlement. That community was Di'hạįį Gwich'in. This is good evidence for cooperation during war and verifies the description of K'ets'eggaagge' that they lived in widely separated family groups and that they had direct contact with the Iñupiat which was a question that interested Zagoskin; (8) Kò'ehdan and Łihteerạhdyaa were their

Di'hąįį Gwich'in names. Their other name/names have been lost. They must have had Iñupiat and Nendaaghe Hʉt'aane Koyukon names; (9) the retaliation party, after preparing the whole summer, left in late August or early September during the fall chum salmon run. Based upon present day chum distribution, the community could have been near the Neek'elehno' (South Fork) of the Koyukuk River. I would discount the Kobuk River because of point number ten; it simply would not have taken the better part of a month to go from the Kobuk River to Point Hope; (10) the trip to the Iñupiat settlement took the better part of a month which brought them there in mid-September or early October about the time that the inland Iñupiat put their *umiaks* up for the winter. If they left the Neek'elehno' (South Fork) and went up the Aalaasuk (Alatna River) to the Noatak then proceeded to the Chukchi Sea, or conversely went up the Eł tsyeeh no' (John River) to the Nunataaq (Noatak) and to the Chukchi Sea, that would have taken the better part of a month; (11) the Neek'elehno' (South Fork) may have been in the Di'hąįį Gwich'in or Too Tleekk'e Hʉt'aane estate, but within Nendaaghe and Too Loghe Hʉt'aane Koyukon range; (12) the Iñupiat settlement was along the shores of a large lake by the ocean; it was foggy and the Iñupiat *umiaks* were cut up; and (13) Khii Choo (Iqaluġraqpak), the Iñupiaq man, came from an area where chum salmon run—either the Noatak or Kobuk rivers, but most likely the Nunataaq (Noatak River).

We know that Kǫ'ehdan died with a Di'hąįį Gwich'in name. He was a member of the Nendaaghe Hʉt'aane Koyukon. He died before the advent of Christianity in the upper Koyukuk River because he did not have a Christian name. Therefore he must have died prior to 1867 but during the 1840s and perhaps during the K'iitł'it/Anaktuvuk Pass battle. His wife, Łihteerąhdyaa, became one of the wives of Dits'ii K'iitł'uu, the Di'hąįį Gwich'in patriarch.[34] Łihteerąhdyaa was a barren woman. She may have been older than Sarah Shaaghan Dik. Łihteerąhdyaa and Sarah Shaaghan Dik were Nendaaghe Hʉt'aane Koyukon who were driven eastward. They first joined the

Too Loghe Hʉt'aane Koyukon, the Di'haįi Gwich'in, and then finally
the Neets'aįi Gwich'in. Sarah Shaaghan Dik may also have lived for
awhile along the upper Kobuk River. They fled down the Eł tsyeeh
no' (John River) and were taken in by Dits'ii K'iitł'uu. To show his
affection, Dits'ii K'iitł'uu renamed her Shiłihteerąhdyaa which
means, "My one whom we take back and forth." She was called
Łihteerąhdyaa because she was taken back and forth among the
Iñupiat, Nendaaghe, and Too Loghe Hʉt'aane Koyukon and the
Di'haįi Gwich'in. Shiłihteerąhdyaa did not have a Christian name,
which means she died before 1867 but after the death of Dits'ii
K'iitł'uu (circa 1855)[35] and the Di'haįi Gwich'in displacement.

The Kǫ'ehdan story is one of the earliest Iñupiat war stories
told by the Neets'aįi Gwich'in. It dates to the 1820s. It found its way
to the Teetł'it Gwich'in of Peel River through the eastward movement
of the Di'haįi Gwich'in after 1850. The story of Dihch'i'ts'ik was
placed in the Kobuk River valley, but the Kǫ'ehdan story is not placed
in that valley. The Nendaaghe Hʉt'aane Koyukon community was
near steep cliffs which could be anywhere in western Nendaaghe,
the headwaters district of the Noatak, Alatna, Nigu, and Etivluk rivers
or it could have been at a settlement along Tukuto, Etivlik, or Atłiq
lakes. Burch estimates that there was a battle at Atłiq Lake (the middle
of the Smith Mountain Lakes) in the mid 1820s.[36] My notion is that
those may have been two separate incidents which occurred within
a year or two of each other and that the attack on the settlement at
Narvaŋuluk (Etivlik Lake) happened first even though it is in the
heart of the Nendaaghe Hʉt'aane Koyukon estate. Kǫ'ehdan fled to
a community which was able to fish along the Koyukuk River and
specifically on or near the Neek'elehno' (South Fork). This
community could have been Neeltugh Tene,* a community near the
mouth of the Neek'elehno' (South Fork). This story suggests that
the Nendaaghe and Too Loghe Hʉt'aane Koyukon were in the habit

---

* Recorded name of that community in Koyukon. It may have been translated from
the Gwich'in original.

of using a *qarġi* (men's house), while the Kodeel Kkaakk'e Hʉt'aane (Kateel River people) of the lower Koyukuk River did not use the *qarġi* during the 1840s—neither did the Neets'ąįį Gwich'in. The Iñupiat community along the northwest Alaska coast was wiped out all except for Kǫ'ehdan's trading partner. Kǫ'ehdan's community was completely wiped out. It has always struck me how much emphasis was placed upon the dialogue in this story. The Iñupiaq warrior, Kǫ'ehdan, his sister-in-law, his trading partner, and the elderly Di'hąįį Gwich'in lady all speak. Each one speaks with the deeper emotional tones of the situations. All these people knew each other intimately. The beginning of the Nendaaghe Hʉt'aane Koyukon displacement from Nendaaghe/Uyaġaaq, the headwaters district of the upper Nunataaq (Noatak River), began with these two decisive battles where a whole community was wiped out on both sides. These conflicts may have been exacerbated by the increase in trade from the Siberians in Hotham Bay and the desire of the Iñupiat to take over the east/west trade route through Nendaaghe/Uyaġaaq. The Kǫ'ehdan story is not just another story of a battle, but the story of an important turning point in the history of the Nendaaghe Hʉt'aane Koyukon displacement and the incursion of the Iñupiat from the north and west.

The retaliation party went to a coastal plain, near a lake, inhabited by Iñupiat. Burch and Mishler have written about the battle at Anaktuvuk Pass and have referenced this event with other events. The first event was the genealogy from Martha Swan, a Nuataaġmiut Iñupiaq (central Noatak) person, whom we shall discuss later. "The second reference point is the massacre of the forty to fifty people in the Iñupiaq village of Nuvuġaluaq on the Chukchi Sea Coast, near Point Hope, by "Indians." "There is no question that the perpetrators were Indians…"[37] If this was the retaliation of Kǫ'ehdan, then the Indians would have been Nendaaghe Hʉt'aane Koyukon along with a few Too Loghe Hʉt'aane Koyukon, Too Tleekk'e Hʉt'aane or Di'hąįį Gwich'in and Saakił Hʉt'aane Koyukon who joined in the attack. The site of this battle was reported by Beechey in September of

1826.[38] However Point Hope and Nuvuġaluaq were explored first
by the Russian explorer M. N. Vasiliev and G. S. Shishmarev on
their 1819–1820 expedition when they reported 600 residents in
two settlements at Point Hope.[39] Burch and Mishler estimated that
forty to fifty people were massacred at Nuvuġaluaq.[40] That means
that the retaliation took place sometime between 1821–1826.

Burch and Mishler went on to say that, "the same Indians
returned the following year. However, this time the raiding party
walked into a trap and was wiped out."[41] Perhaps Kọ'ehdan died
then. Given the second attack, this would suggest that the Nendaaghe,
Saakił, and Too Loghe Hut'aane Koyukon along with the Di'hąįį
Gwich'in, who joined in the attack, recouped and made preparations
for the following year. They must have held joint hunting, fishing,
and gathering efforts for the year leading up to the second attack.
They had to lay food aside for their families and for themselves
upon their return. The question arises, why would the Di'hąįį
Gwich'in go out of their way to help the Nendaaghe, Saakił, and
Too Loghe Hut'aane Koyukon in an area way out of their estate and
range, and not just for one year, but for two consecutive years? The
direct distance between Point Hope and the Neek'elehno' (South
Fork) is approximately 260 miles. I think the Di'hąįį Gwich'in joined
for three reasons: (1) they lived and hunted on the north slope, (2)
therefore, they looked upon the Iñupiat incursion onto the Nendaaghe
and Too Loghe estates as a threat to their adjoining estate to the
east, and (3) they were, through generations, interrelated with the
northern Koyukon. The Di'hąįį Gwich'in who lived above the Eł
tsyeeh no' (John River) probably had more reason to join since it
was within their range that the Iñupiat incursion was a real threat. A
few men probably hired on as mercenaries. Burch and Mishler
estimated this battle to have occurred sometime in the 1820s, the
same time period as my independent estimate of the Kọ'ehdan
retaliation. Both retaliations took place between 1821 and 1826. The
massacre at Nuvuġaluaq, a suburb of Point Hope, was no doubt led
by Kọ'ehdan.

If Burch and Mishler are right about the return party being wiped out, this would have been a major blow for the Nendaaghe Hut'aane Koyukon. First a community massacred which led to a retaliation war party, and then all the returning warriors being wiped out by the Iñupiat. Then, secondly, the battle at Atłiq Lake. It may have been after these defeats (1821–26) that the young Sayyen fled to the central Kobuk and was taken in by his Akuniġmiut Iñupiat family. As stated earlier this may also have coincided with a shortage of caribou or famine. For a widely disbursed nation of hunter-gatherers (estimated total population of 520^{42})[*] to lose fifty or even thirty warriors would have been devastating. There simply were not enough men to defend the former territory or to hunt for the remaining women, children, and elderly. The only thing to do was to flee eastward to join the Too Loghe Hut'aane Koyukon family groups. We know that at least one band of the Nendaaghe Hut'aane Koyukon went southward to the Kobuk River. I postulate that they moved southward in larger numbers than eastward initially. This suggests that the Nendaaghe Hut'aane/Uyaġaaġmiut remained in the vicinity of Nendaaghe, even after the defeats of the 1820s, and did not move northward and eastward until after the late 1830s-early 1840s defeat in the upper Kobuk River valley. That would be a period of thirteen to twenty years.

I want to return to the Martha Swan genealogy (Fig. 13) and to include Della Keats' genealogy as well. This will help to estimate the time of the famine in Nendaaghe, the upper Nunataaq (Noatak River). From Martha's genealogy we can see that the time of her grandfather's birth was estimated to be about 1840 which would have been about the end of the famine period (1820–30s). That would

---

[*] Taking Krech's total estimated population of the Gwich'in people before contact (1750) at 5400 and dividing the number by nine Gwich'in nations equals 600 per nation. Burch estimates the population of the Kuuvaum Kaŋiaġmiut Iñupiat to be 650 in 1870, the Nuataaġmiut population to be 535 in 1800, and the Uyaġaaġmiut to between 250–300. Therefore, I estimate the Nendaaghe Hut'aane Koyukon population to be 520 before 1820.

Fig. 13. Genealogy of Martha Swan and Della Keats demonstrating the
presence of Koyukon in the upper Noaktak during the 1840s. Courtesy of
Ernest S. Burch, Jr.

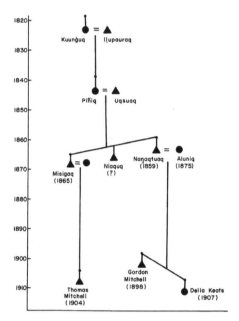

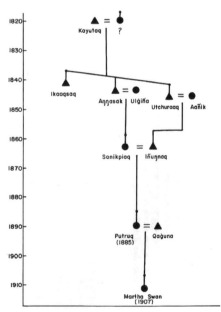

have been after the Nendaaghe Hut'aane Koyukon displacement from the upper Kobuk River, but during their last years in Nendaaghe.

Now we can mention other oral accounts of Uyaġaaġmiut (Nendaaghe Hut'aane Koyukon) presence in the Nendaaghe/ Uyaġaaq estate from the northen Iñupiaq perspective. Here I would like to name all the Iñupiat informants from the northwestern arctic area who have through their oral tradition passed on their history and, through association, the history of the Nendaaghe, Saakił, and Too Loghe Hut'aane Koyukon: David Nuntak[43] Adams, Ezra Kumak[44] Booth, John Patkuraq[45] Brown, Mark Uluchiaq[46] Cleveland, Robert Nasruk Cleveland, Charlie Pigliġiaq Custer, Herbert Qutana Custer, Tommy Paankaliaq Douglas, Frank Kutvak[47] Glover, Jenny Masruana Jackson, Della Putyak Keats, Edith Puptuan[48] Kennedy, Charlie Qiñugana[49] Lee, Levi Alasuk[50] Mills, Thomas Uqsruġaaluk[51] Mitchell, Agnes Smith, Suzie Aniġniq Wood (White) Stocking, Charlotte Saviugan[52] Swan, Martha H. Swan, Joe Immałuraq Sun, and Charlie Uluġaaġruk Wood.

From the northern and eastern informants, Dikajaw, Simon Panniaq Paneak, Sarah Shaaghan Dik, Johnny Frank, Henry T'ąąval Williams, and Steven Tsee Gho' Tsyaa Tsal Peter, Sr., and previous accounts, we have the following picture of western Nendaaghe. The Nendaaghe Hut'aane Koyukon lived in the estate known as Nendaaghe(Iyaġaaq/Uyaġaaq), therefore the inhabitants were known to the Iñupiat as Iyaġaaġmiut along the Kobuk River, Uyaġaaġmiut to the north, and perhaps Nunataaġmiut in Barrow, Alaska. It is not known what the Gwich'in people to the east called the Nendaaghe Hut'aane Koyukon, however their name for the neighboring Too Loghe Hut'aane Koyukon was K'iitł'it Gwich'in. They spoke the Koyukon language and some also spoke the languages of their neighbors. The Nendaaghe and Too Loghe Hut'aane Koyukon lived at the headwaters of the Noatak, Alatna, Colville, and John rivers and around Interior lakes (Chandler, Kurupa, Tulugaq, Tukuto, Etivlik, and Atłiq) in stone houses. They traveled further northward on a seasonal basis to Kurupa Lake and beyond to trade along the coast. They resided in the area between approximately post 1250 and 1850. Along the Noatak they were known to inhabit the area at least above the Anigaak (Anuik River[53]) and definitely above Ataongarak Creek.[54] The Nendaaghe Hut'aane Koyukon were closely related to all their nearest neighbors, the Saakił Hut'aane Koyukon, the Akuniġmiut Iñupiat along the Kobuk River, the Nuataaġmiut Iñupiat of the central Noatak valley, the Kuukpiġmiut Iñupiat (Qaŋmaliġmiut, Killiġmiut, and Kaŋianiġmiut bands) in the Kuukpik (Colville River) headwaters, the Too Loghe Hut'aane Koyukon and Di'haii Gwich'in to the east, and southeast to the Koyukon of the middle Koyukuk River valley.

The Uyaġaaġmiut were known to live in stone houses, to use qarġi or men's house, to build stone and willow caribou corals, and *iñuksuich*[*] (stone piles or pillars used to drive the caribou into the coral) (Figs. 14, 15, 16). Sometime around 1820 the first Nendaaghe Hut'aane Koyukon community was massacred by the Iñupiat. This took place on the Nendaaghe estate, perhaps at Narvaŋuluk (Etivlik

Fig. 14. Caribou corral near Chandler Lake. Photo by Grant Spearman.

---

* *Iñuksuk* singular, *iñuksuich* plural.

Fig. 15. Rocks along a caribou corral at Chandler Lake. Photo by Grant Spearman.

Fig. 16. Stone cache near Chandler Lake. Photo by Grant Spearman.

Lake) and definitely at Atłiq Lake. The Iñupiat attacked from the north and south, maybe simultaneously, or in successive years. The conflict may have been brought on by the increase in demand for trade items from the Bering Straits and pressure from the Nuataaġmiut and Tikiġaġmiut (Point Hope nation)[55] Iñupiat to the west and the Kuukpiġmiut to the north who wanted to dominate that trade route. The Koyukon retaliation party wiped out the community of Nuvuġaluaq, a suburb of Point Hope, Alaska between 1821–26. Colder weather conditions prevailed beginning in 1800. There was a famine which encompassed most of the Interior northwest during the 1820s and 1830s. Conflicts continued in northern and southern Nendaaghe. This would suggest that during the 1820s and 30s the upper Kobuk River was full of destitute refugees both from the Nunataaq (Noatak) and maybe from the middle Koyukuk rivers. An enclave of Nendaaghe Hut'aane Koyukon was founded in the upper Kobuk. The Nendaaghe Hut'aane Koyukon were expelled from the upper Kobuk during the early 1840s. Most of the men, Iñupiat and Koyukon, were bilingual up to that time. After the early 1840s the Saakił Hut'aane Koyukon adopted the Iñupiat language, lost their Nendaaghe Hut'aane Koyukon contacts, and stopped being bilingual. By the time of the lost hunters the central Kobuk River men had lost their bilingualism. It was the elderly Nendaaghe or Too Loghe Hut'aane Koyukon man who communicated with them through sign language. That was just before 1860. The Nendaaghe Hut'aane/Uyaġaaġmiut acquired a reputation for being troublemakers and warring with their neighbors. By the mid 1840s the Nendaaghe Hut'aane Koyukon were completely gone from western Nendaaghe, the upper Noatak specifically.

Kuukpik, Kuukpiġmiut, and the Northern Borders

The Nendaaghe Hut'aane Koyukon (Uyaġaaġmiut) presence in the upper Kuukpik (Colville River) has been documented by Dr. John Simpson as previously stated. However, before we can address the Nendaaghe and Too Loghe Hut'aane Koyukon presence we need to establish the Kuukpiġmiut estate. Burch stated "the most distinctive nation in northwestern Alaska was the one whose estate was along the Colville River, Kuukpiġmiut. In this district, resources were clustered in three widely separated patches...the members of this nation were divided into three regional bands, one per patch. Beginning on the upriver end, these were known as the Kaŋianiġmiut, the Killiġmiut, and the Qaŋmaliġmiut, respectively."[56] That means the Kaŋianiġmiut or "headwaters people"[57] who were centered around the Itivliim Kuuŋa (Etivluk River) and Alaasuurak (Nigu River), the Killiġmiut[58] or "the people of the edge of the mountains" of the Killik River, and the Qaŋmaliġmiut[59] or "people of the farthest in region" of the Kaŋmalik (Anaktuvuk River.) The Nunataaġmiut (Nu-na-tan'g-meun), if they existed at all as a nation, lived to the west of the Kaŋianiġmiut regional band along the Colville River.[60] However, Maguire noted the following, "Doctor Simpson thinks the Nunata gives to the inhabitants residing on it the name of Nunatagmun who have hitherto puzzled him."[61] It would stand to reason that the Nunataaġmiut would be residents of the Nunataaq (Noatak). However the upper Nunataaq (Noatak) residents just below the headwaters are currently known as the Nuataaġmiut Iñupiat. Burch questioned whether or not the Nunataaġmiut were a group at all. Perhaps this could be the older pronunciation of Nunamiut, which generally means inland dwellers or it could have been the Point Barrow Iñupiat name for residents of Nendaaghe in 1854. I will take Dr. Simpson's lead and regard that group as the Nuataaġmiut Iñupiat of the upper Noatak River, who by that time would have taken over the abandoned Nendaaghe estate. The Ulumiut Iñupiat[62] or "people from women's knife" are a fourth band who lived in the Itkillik River or Ulu valley as it is also known. The Ulumiut Iñupiat, however, were established only after the total displacement of the Di'hạịị Gwich'in and Koyukon in the Itkillik River area after circa 1847.

Now we can review Simpson's statement of 1854 and interject Iñupiat, Koyukon, and Gwich'in names: "The inland Equimaux

[Kuukpiġmiut (Kaŋianiġmiut, Killiġmiut, and Qaŋmaliġmiut regional bands) and Nuataaġmiut Iñupiat] also call them Ko'-yu-kan, and divide them into three sections or tribes, two of which they know, and say they have different modes of dancing. One is called [Nendaaghe and Too Loghe Hʉt'aane Koyukon (aka K'iitł'it Gwich'in)] and inhabits the [Itkillik River],...the second, [Dih'ạįį Gwich'in], whose country is further south;..."[63] Nothing could be more correct for 1854. That was at least nine years after the Nendaaghe and Too Loghe Hʉt'aane Koyukon displacement in the upper Kuukpik (Colville). They merged with the Di'hạįį and Neets'ạįį Gwich'in sometime during the mid-1840s.[64] The Nuataaġmiut Iñupiat and Kuukpiġmiut Iñupiat took over the important east-west trade route that ran through the former Nendaaghe/Uyaġaaq estate of the Nendaaghe Hʉt'aane Koyukon. It is important to note that they did not distinguish between the Nendaaghe and Too Loghe Hʉt'aane Koyukon.

To establish the boundaries we will turn to oral sources. The late Samuel Kunaknana (born 1913) of Barrow, Alaska stated that; "At the time, our forefathers [Kuukpiġmiut] lived inland around the Kuukpiq (Colville River) area. But also, the Indians [Uyaġaaġmiut] inhabited Anaktuvuk [Pass]; During spring, our forefathers traveled to Anaktuvuk and visited with their relatives. They would visit but would always return..."[65] This confirms contact and familiarity through intermarriage between the two groups. Elijah Kakiññaaq Kakinya (born 1895) of Anaktuvuk Pass said, "It is said that Indians lived there at Anaktuvuk Pass before; also there were the Eskimos [Kaŋianiġmiut and Killiġmiut regional bands and Nuataaġmiut] who traveled downriver through Kuukpik [Colville]...they 'intermarried' with the Indians in those days...It is said that eventually the Indians were killed. After the fighting was over, the rest of the Indians fled up east. The others they stayed where Indians had lived before*."[66]

---

* Emphasis added.

Here we have two men who place Kuukpiġmiut borders and boundaries in the upper Colville River region and distinguish between the Kuukpiq estate and that of Nendaaghe, which was definitely in the mountains. The Nendaaghe/Too Loghe estates were in the mountains all along the Kuukpik (upper Colville) from the Itivliim Kuuŋa (Etivluk River) to Kaŋmalik (Anaktuvuk River.) According to Gubser, the Indians had settlements on the Killik, Okokmilaga, Chandler, Anaktuvuk, and Itkillik rivers.[67] The Indians on the Itkillik River would have been the Di'hạii Gwich'in and not the Koyukon. That was the northern border and boundary of the Nendaaghe and Too Loghe Hut'aane Koyukon and Di'hạii Gwich'in along the Itkillik River. Kakinya, however, interjected the notion that the Uyaġaaġmiut went into an area where other Indians had lived before, but were not there when the Uyaġaaġmiut took over their former estate. That is, the Nendaaghe and Too Loghe Hut'aane Koyukon moved into an area outside of their own estates. Essentially, this corroborates the Sarah Shaaghan Dik and Shiłihteerạhdyaa stories and other Neets'ạii Gwich'in accounts of transition from the Nendaaghe/Too Loghe estates into the Di'hạii estate.

Part 2, Chapter Notes

1. Nicholas J. Gubser, *"Comparative Study of the Intellectual Culture of the Nunamiut Eskimos at Anaktuvuk Pass, Alaska,"* (Fairbanks: University of Alaska, 1961): 82.

2. Simon Paneak, tape 842, transcript, 1971: 1–3.

3. Burch, personal communication, 1999.

4. Gubser (1961): 82.

5. Edwin S. Hall, Jr., "Kutchin Athapaskan/Nunamiut Eskimo Conflict," *Alaska Journal*, 5, no. 4 (1975): 248.

6. Ernest S. Burch, Jr., and Craig W. Mishler, "The Di'haįi Gwich'in: Mystery People of Northern Alaska," *Arctic Anthropology* 32, no. 1 (1995), 152.

7. Robert Gal, personal communication. 1999.

8. Justus Mekiana, Killik River Data, tape 11:6, trans. Grant Spearman, 4 May 1990.

9. Helge Ingstad, *Nunamiut Unipkaaŋich told by Elijah Kakinya and Simon Paneak Collected by Helge Ingstad*, ed. and trans. Knut Bergsland (Barrow, Alaska: The North Slope Borough History, Language, and Culture, 1987): 353.

10. Ernest S. Burch, Jr., *Iñupiaq Eskimo Nations of Northwest Alaska*, (Fairbanks: University of Alaska Press, 1998c): 98–100.

11. Ronald O. Skoog, "Ecology of the Caribou in Alaska," (Ph.D. diss., University of California, Berkeley, 1968): 305.

12. Burch (1998b): 111.

13. Ibid.: 111.

14. Ibid.: 79.

15. Burch (1998b): 117.

16. Ibid.

17. Burch (1998b): 111.

18. Burch, and Mishler (1995): pp. 147–172.

19. Burch (1998a): 19–48, 1998b.

20. Edwin S. Hall, Jr., "Speculation on the Late Prehistory of the Kutchin Athapaskans," *Ethnohistory* 16 (4) (1969): 317–333.

21. Hall (1975): 248–252.

22. Gubser (1961): 81.

23. Helge Ingstad, *Nunamiut*, (New York: W. W. Norton & Company, 1954).

24. Johnny and Sarah Frank, *Neerihiinjik: We Traveled From Place to Place*, ed. Craig Mishler (Fairbanks: Alaska Native Language Center, University of Alaska Fairbanks, 1995): map on page xxix.

25. Steven Tsee Gho', Tsyaa Tsal Peter, Sr., personal communication, 1987–97. This reference will be shortened to STP, 1987–97 throughout this text.

26. Grant Spearman, personal communication, 1998.

27. McDonald, journal entry, 12 March 1967.

28. See also Richard Slobodin, "Without Fire: A Kutchin Tale Of Warfare, Survival, and Vengence" in proceedings: Northern Athapaskan Conference, Vol. 1, National Museum of Man Mercury Series, Canadian Ethnology Service Paper No. 27, 1971: 260–301.

29. Katherine Peter, personal communication, 1999.

30. Henry Williams, *Kǫ'ehdan*, trans. Moses P. Gabriel (Fairbanks: Alaska Native Language Center, University of Alaska Fairbanks, n.d.).

31. Loreena Williams, personal communication, 1999.

32. Maguire (1988): 2.

33. Zagoskin (1967): 152.

34. STP, 1987–97.

35. Indian Balances Sheet, dated 1855, Hudson's Bay Company Archives, B240/a/8.

36. Burch (1998a): 26.

37. Burch and Mishler (1995): 158.

38. Frederick William Beechey, *Narrative of a Voyage to the Pacific and Beering's Strait, To Cooperate With The Polar Expedition, in the years 1825, 26, 27, 28,* 2nd ed. (New York: Henry Colburn and Richard Bertley, 1968): 451, 452.

39. J. R. Bockstoce, *Eskimos of Northwest Alaska In The Early Nineteenth Century,* Monograph Series No. 1 (University of Oxford, Pitt Rivers Museum, Oxprint Limited Oxford, 1977): 7.

40. Burch and Mishler (1995): 158.

41. Ibid.

42. Shepard Krech, III, "On The Aboriginal Population of the Kutchin," *Arctic Anthropology*, XV-1, 1978: 98; Burch (1998b): 117, 138; Burch, *International Affairs* VII (1998): 7.

43. Edna Commack, personal communication, June 1999.

44. Burch (1998b): 337.

45. Ibid.: 333.

46. Edna Commack, personal communication, 1999.

47. Burch (1998b): 333.

48. Linda Piquk Lee, Ruthie Tatqaviñ Sampson and Edward Tennant, eds., *Lore of the Iñupiat, Vol. 3* (Alaska: Northwest Arctic Borough School District, 1992): 285.

49. Burch (1998b): 332.

50. Ibid.: 333.

51. Ibid.

52. Ibid.

53. Della Keats, Burch field notes, 1969(c): 43.

54. Burch (1998b): 111.

55. Ernest S. Burch, Jr., *The Traditional Eskimo Hunters Of Point Hope, Alaska: 1800–1875* (Barrow, Alaska: The North Slope Borough, 1981).

56. Burch (1998c): 29, 33.

57. Grant Spearman, *kaŋianiq,* "the root or the source," personal communication; Loreena Williams, "closest to mainland," personal communication, June 1999.

58. Grant Spearman, *killiq,* "the edge," personal communication; Loreena Williams, "in back, to the edge of the mountains," personal communication, June 1999.

59. Grant Spearman, *qaŋmaliq,* "farthest in," personal communication; Loreena Williams, "more inland," personal communication, June 1999.

60. Burch (1998a): 25–26.

61. Rochfort Maguire, *The Journal of Rochfort Maguire 1853–1854*, ed. John Bockstoce (London: The Hakluyt Society, 1988): 306.

62. Grant Spearman, personal communication, group name; Loreena Williams, *ulu,* "women's knife," personal communication, June 1999.

63. Maguire (1988): 543.

64. STP (1987–97). This information will be presented later.

65. Flossie Hopson, North Slope Elders Conference, Barrow, Alaska, 22–26 May 1978: 46.

66. Ibid.

67. Gubser (1961): 83.

Part III

Related Archaelogy & Oral Tradition

Related Archaeology
and Oral Tradition

There are archaeological sites both north and south of the Brooks Range running from west to east. Most of these sites are around large inland lakes, in the passes, and in the river valleys. There are problems relating these sites to the Late Prehistoric times because often times dating is difficult and sometimes there are only a few artifacts at a site which make it almost impossible to assign the assemblage to a specific tool industry. However, the Iñupiat have attributed many stone houses, stone blinds, caribou corals, meat caches, and *iñuksuich* (rock cairns) to the Indians.[1] I have mentioned Tukuto, Narvaŋuluk (Etivlik), Kikitaliorak, Kipmik, Kinyiksukvik, and Kurupa lakes in western and northern Nendaaghe and Batza Tèna, the source of obsidian for most of the central Brooks Range, located along the middle Koyukuk River. Now we can turn our attention to the central Brooks Range from Klo-kut (Tłoo kat, upon the grass) (G), which is a known Gwich'in site to the east of our study area long the upper Porcupine River, westward to Chandler Lake (Narvaqvak).[2]

Tłoo kat (Klo-kut) is located in northwestern Yukon Territory, Canada. In regard to the tool assemblage at Tłoo kat (Klo-kut) Richard E. Morlan says, "Relationships between the Klo-kut materials and assemblages recovered from other areas of northwestern North America can be identified only tentatively at the present time…The strongest ties appear to lie to the west along the Brooks Range. These links reach as far as the Kobuk River with intervening cross-ties in a few sites along the Yukon River, in Anaktuvuk Pass, and in the Sagavanirktok valley."[3] Morlan elaborates upon this point further, "Many sites in Western Alaska have yielded a wide range of artifacts which resemble Klo-kut materials quite closely, but most of the comparisons are with sites attributed to late prehistoric and historic Eskimo occupations."[4] Many sites north of the Brooks Range, especially in Ulu Valley [Itkillik River Valley] have not been dated and very often there are not enough artifacts to identify with an assemblage of tools.[5] To continue with Morlan's Tłoo kat (Klo-kut) paper he says that "Similarites between portions of the Nunamiut Eskimo bone industry and that at Klo-kut were already mentioned, but one site in Anaktuvuk Pass requires special mention for several reasons. The Kavik site (Campbell 1962: 48–49;[6] 1968[7]) is the only locality yet discovered in Alaska or the Yukon in which nearly every artifact has a close counterpart at Klo-kut...no other site had yielded points so similar to the Klo-kut specimens, particularly to those which characterize the Late Prehistoric period...On the basis of these similarities Campbell (1968[8]) now regards Kavik as a possible representative of a pre-Nunamiut, Athabaskan link for Anaktuvuk Pass..."[9] The tool assemblage at Tłoo kat (Klo-kut) demonstrates an Athabascan link for Anaktuvuk Pass sites in the Late Prehistoric times.

Herbert L. Alexander surveyed the Atigun Valley and the Narvaqvak (Chandler Lake) area in the early 1960s. He also was at the Putu site on the Sagavanirktok River. Most of the material at the Putu site was dated earlier than Late Prehistoric, however, Alexander commented "The use of Batza Tena obsidian from the other side of the Brooks Range extends the range considerably beyond mere local knowledge."[10] Batza Tèna obsidian was traded extensively to the north and east of the middle Koyukuk River for at least the last 8,000 to 11,000 years before present and has been found at sites dating back for 1,000 years.[11] At Narvaqvak (Chandler Lake)

Alexander found, "14 sites including circular structures of piled stones, a stone cache, 11 tent rings, two caribou coral drives and three chipping stations."[12] Many of these sites were said to come from the Indians by the Anaktuvuk Pass residents. While in the Atigun valley Alexander once asked Panniaq, who served as informant, if he knew of other Indian sites, "Paneak's reply included mention of passing through the north end of the Atigun Valley and that there were; pit houses there at Galbraith Lake." Alexander's discoveries at Narvaqvak (Chandler Lake) and in the Atigun Valley were familiar sights to the Anaktuvuk Pass residents.

Starting in 1969, Edwin S. Hall, Jr. wrote several articles about the Kutchin presence in the central Brooks Range.[13] Hall "equated Kavik for Dihai, or Kutchin occupation of the Anaktuvuk Pass area because Kavik projectile points are similar to those known from Klo-kut,...The form of the late prehistoric Koyukon projectile points is unknown; they may be similar to those known from Kavik and Klo-kut. This issue aside there is no historical evidence that the Koyukon Athapaskans ever entered the Brooks Range proper. The timbered southern flanks appear to have been a buffer zone between them and the Nunamiut, penetrated only occasionally by the latter."[14] The Koyukuk projectile point is not well defined, however there have been a few Kavik points that were found at Coldfoot, Alaska, along the Middle Fork (Tlakołnika,[15] Hʉkkughutne, Hʉkkughutno'*)[16] of the Koyukuk River and on the Jim River (Noon kuhno'†)[17] up the Neek'elehno' (South Fork).[18] In another article about the Brooks Range prehistory, Hall presented some very valuable information: "the Killik River appears to be a north-south dividing line in terms of house types, with semi-subterranean houses the norm to the west and ground level winter houses the only type represented in the east."[19] Hall went into detail about the differences between

---

* Hʉkkughutne, Hʉkkughutno' means "swift water river."
† Noon Kuhno' means "big animal (bear) river," "big porcupine river." Big porcupine is used here as a circumlocution for naming the big animal (brown bear).

Fig. 17. Drawing by Lewis Binford of Tulugaq Lake. North side of
Anaktuvuk Pass.

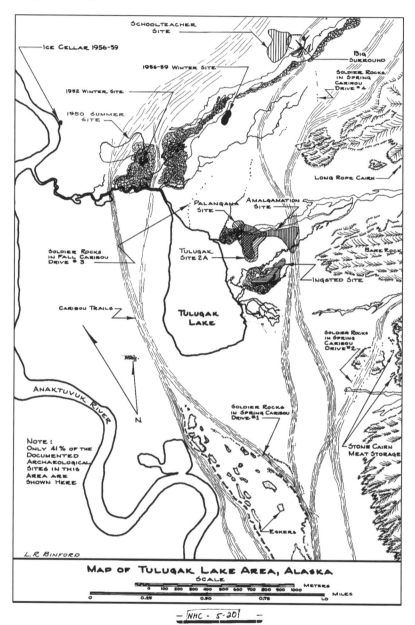

MAP OF TULUGAK LAKE AREA, ALASKA

the "Western and Eastern Nunamiut" and said that, "The former are characterized by a large population, extensive use of pottery, relatively permanent winter villages with semi-subterranean houses of several types and large, well constructed *kariyit* [plural of *karġi**]. The Eastern Nunamiut utilized ground level willow frame-caribou skin tents for housing, a larger version of the same as a *karigi†* and, apparently, did not use much pottery."[20] Hall also elaborated on house types elsewhere.[21] Hall's early papers about the Gwich'in presence in the western Brooks Range were speculative and probing, however, he opened the field of investigation for others and laid down a solid foundation for the present work.

In Anaktuvuk Pass there are many sites that are attributed to the Indians. Kanŋumavik (gathering place[22]), a campsite about three or four miles to the north of Anaktuvuk Pass is said to be a site where the Iñupiat and Uyaġaaġmiut spent several seasons together before their final confrontation. The area north and south of Tulugaq Lake have stone house pits attributed to the "little people," a caribou coral, *iñuksuich* (stone cairns), numerous stone cache pits, stone hunting blinds, and a small knoll thought to be a burial site (Fig. 17). The Indians were said to be camping just to the north of Tulugaq Lake when their last big battle was fought. Considering that archaeological remains of the Indians are strewn about the landscape as they are, it is not surprising that the oral tradition of the Iñupiat of Anaktuvuk Pass is rich with stories about the Indians.

Continuation of Koyukon Displacement

Now to get a picture of how the Nendaaghe and Too Loghe Hut'aane Koyukon were displaced we turn again to Simon Paneak (Fig. 18). Panniaq says, "And Indians moving from there [Saakił and southern Nendaaghe estates] to the northern Brooks Range near

---

* Another spelling of *qarġi*, men's house.
† Another variant spelling of *qarġi*.

Fig. 18. Panniaq Family Tree.

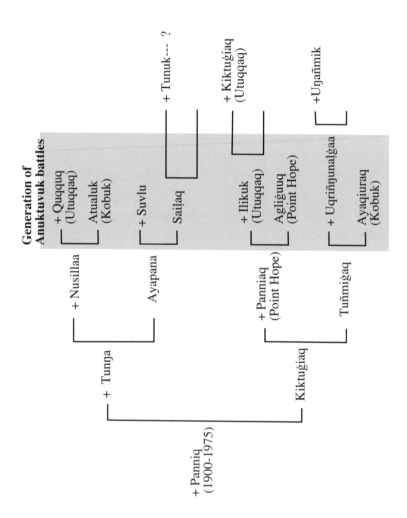

Howard Pass, over there where the Eskimo [Kuukiġmiut] and Nunamiut* [Inland dwellers] were too and stayed over there for a long time and same thing when the Indians grow up they became an unfriendly people and jealous on the ground."²³ Here Panniaq is talking about the Nendaaghe Hʉt'aane Koyukon interaction with the Kaŋianigmiut regional band—the people who lived along the lower Itivliim Kuuŋa (Etivluk River)—but he also included the Killiġmiut and Qaŋmaliġmiut regional bands to the east when he said "Nunamiut" (inland dwellers). To be more specific, Justus Mekiana stated that the Kaŋianigmiut band were just below Itilyiargiok Creek (Itgiliagiaq, "the way to the Indians") along the upper Aalaasuuraq (Nigu River).²⁴ It is possible that the Nendaaghe Hʉt'aane Koyukon still had possession of Tukuto Lake at this point. As of the late 1830s and early 1840s the Nendaaghe Hʉt'aane Koyukon were both to the north and east of Howard Pass, and in the upper Nunataaq (Noatak), whereas the Too Loghe Hʉt'aane Koyukon were in the Aalaasuk (Alatna River) drainage well within their own estate.

It appears from the forgoing account (and previous indications) that all the Nendaaghe Hʉt'aane Koyukon did not flee to the upper Kobuk River. It may have been one band of the Nendaaghe Hʉt'aane Koyukon who were living in the upper Kobuk and the remainder continued to stay at Tukuto Lake and the area to the east of Howard Pass. Meanwhile the upper Aalaasuk (Alatna River) Too Loghe Hʉt'aane Koyukon maintained their northern estate. They did not move. Justus Mekiana maintains that the Uyaġaaġmiut were living along the Aalaasuk (Alatna River) at the time. It was during this same period that there was persistent conflict with the Nuataaġmiut Iñupiat to the west. I have come to the conclusion that some of the

---

* Nunamiut with a capital letter is the twentieth century name for the people of Anaktuvuk Pass, Alaska. Panniaq, no doubt, was using the term generically, since at the time of his narrative there were no Nunamiut at Anaktuvuk Pass. The transcriber capitalized the word.

Fig. 19. Justus Mekiana. Photo by Grant Spearman.

Nuataaġmiut Iñupiat conflicts with the upper Kobuk River people transpired with the Nendaaghe Hut'aane Koyukon who were refugees in that area. Burch estimates that the Uyaġaaġmiut probably abandoned the Headwaters District during the 1840s.[25] On this point we do agree, the upper Nunataaq (Noatak) and Kuukpik (Colville) rivers were abandoned by the resident Athabascan group during the 1840s.

    Panniaq presented reasons for the conflicts which arose: (1) "And Eskimo...they could kill all the animals, as much as they could catch but Indians (didn't)—Indian they love to take a limit because sounds like to me they are smart people they don't want to kill all the animals...(where)ever they used to live, they thought it might be, they might have animals for next year, for future..., and (2) "They stayed together sometime over there in upper Colville, some young guys or women married to get the wives from Indian and some Indians got wives from Eskimo and during that stay together for so many years...they became unfriendly (with) each other."[26]

The first reason given is that the Iñupiat wanted to kill more caribou than the Nendaaghe Hʉt'aane Koyukon thought appropriate, since it was within their estate that caribou were being harvested in the first place. But if we recall, the Nendaaghe Hʉt'aane Koyukon were initially in Nendaaghe in larger numbers until the first major defeats circa 1820. It was after the major defeats somewhere along the southern upper Nunataaq (Noatak) boundaries and Atłiq Lake in the north, with their numbers lowered, that the subsequent conflicts occurred. Their neighbors, recognizing their vulnerability, began to encroach upon their estate, take more caribou, and to exhibit more aggression toward the Nendaaghe Hʉt'aane Koyukon. This may have coincided with a caribou shortage which most likely began in the 1820s and persisted through to the 1840s. Grant Spearman has suggested that the Uyaġaaġmiut, being more familiar with their resources, may have had self-imposed limits on their caribou take. The famine of the 1820s and 1830s on the Koyukuk River must have extended northward into Nendaaghe as evidenced by comments from the genealogy of Della Keats and Martha Swan. It would also make sense that if the Nendaaghe Hʉt'aane Koyukon were still living in Nendaaghe year round, they would want to reduce the take of other groups who came into the area on a seasonal basis and especially during years when the caribou were in a low cycle. The intrusion of the Kaŋianiġmiut regional band into the upper Aalaasuuraq (Nigu River) and the seasonal sheep and caribou hunt of the Akuniġmiut Iñupiat (central Kobuk) and the Saakił Hʉt'aane Koyukon (upper Kobuk) from the south must all have been demoralizing for the Nendaaghe Hʉt'aane Koyukon.

Although the Nendaaghe natural resources were limited, the Kuukpiġmiut Iñupiat, I believe, lived in a much more marginal area for natural resources than the Koyukon. The caribou passed through both regions in the fall and spring, but the caribou were forced through constrained passes on their way southward and northward in Nendaaghe which made them easier to harvest. Also, as stated earlier, a major east-west trade route went through Nendaaghe giving residents the coveted role of middlemen. The Kuukpiq* estate simply had fewer resources and with the constant specter of famine, the rate of female infanticide may have been higher among the Kuukpiġmiut Iñupiat. During times of famine young girls and women were more apt to die, since men and boys were fed before the women and children. The Koyukon, no doubt, had a lower incidence of female infanticide, therefore the resulting shortage of women among the Kuukpiġmiut Iñupiat could account for their desire to marry Koyukon women and in one instance to become co-husbands with one woman.[27] It would also explain their reluctance to allow Iñupiat women to marry Koyukon men. It was not a matter of choice, the Kuukpiġmiut had a shortage of women—especially during years of scarcity. Relations were fine when the Koyukon were numerous and they could afford to marry off their women to the Kuukpiġmiut, but under stress and with their numbers depleted, conflict began to fester.

Naturally the conflicts began to increase. As Panniaq says, "...and then finally they begin to fight and in the map Alik Lake...[Atłiq, Nendaaghe Hʉt'aane Koyukon verses Kaŋianiġmiut regional band and perhaps Nuataaġmiut Iñupiat]...and then (they) cannot stay right over there and moving over towards east, like over in Killik [River] and Chandler Lake...staying there for so many years and probably here in Anaktuvuk too. But same thing, they can not stand it no longer they [Kuukpiġmiut] want to fight them [Koyukon] out, and

---

* Kuukpik is the Colville River, Kuukpiq is the estate.

chase them out from country...

"I know over (at) Killik [River] they had...fight, Indian [Uyaġaaġmiut] lose,...20 men and the Eskimo [Killiġmiut regional band] lose 6 people...4 women and 2 men, Eskimo [Killiġmiut band] lose that much but Indian [Uyaġaaġmiut] lost a lot of them."[28]

In this section Panniaq plainly outlines the eastward withdrawal of the Nendaaghe and Too Loghe Hʉt'aane Koyukon along the northern Nendaaghe/Too Loghe estates moving from the Itivliim Kuuŋa (Etivluk River) to the Killik River. Atłiq is located just west of the lower Itivliim Kuuŋa (Etivluk River), the middle of the Smith Mountain Lakes.[29] As stated earlier Burch estimates this battle at Atłiq to have taken place in the mid-1820s. This battle was in the same time-frame as the Kò'ehdan battle that took place in the early 1820s quite possibly at Narvaŋuluk (Etivlik Lake) or in the upper Nunataaq (Noatak). This raises the question of when the community at Tukuto Lake could have been displaced, since it is situated between Narvaŋuluk (Etivlik Lake) and Atłiq along the Itivliim Kuuŋa (Etivluk River), to the west of the upper Aalaasuuraq (Nigu River), and to the north of Howard Pass. The settlement at Narvaŋuluk (Etivlik Lake) and Tukuto lakes were large communities. The estimated abandonment dates for Tukuto Lake (1850) is later than the date of Narvaŋuluk (Etivlik Lake) which is 1700. The estimated dates for Narvaŋuluk (Etivlik Lake) could also be 100 years too early depending on the dating technique; if so, Narvaŋuluk (Etivlik Lake) was abandoned about 1800. At least one band of the Nendaaghe Hʉt'aane Koyukon then temporaritly abandoned Nendaaghe, went south, and returned for the seasonal hunt for a number of years. That particular Nendaaghe Hʉt'aane Koyukon band was permanently routed from the upper Kobuk River in the late 1830s or early 1840s. Given this information the battle at Atłiq occurred during the mid-1820s, as Burch estimates, and opened the way for the Kaŋianiġmiut regional band to move up the Aalaasuuraq (Nigu River). That means the Iñupiat were already there for a good twenty years when the Nendaaghe Hʉt'aane Koyukon band was ousted from the upper Kobuk. In which case, it would have appeared to younger Kaŋianiġmiut that they (the Koyukon) were intruding onto their hunting grounds. Meanwhile, it seems they were living quite peacefully with the Nendaaghe Hʉt'aane Koyukon who may still have been living in the area of Tukuto Lake.

There is one related incident in regard to timing of the Nendaaghe and Too Loghe Hʉt'aane Koyukon displacement. That would be the account of Omigaloon who told Maguire and Simpson, in 1854, that his son (who was about ten years old) was Koyukon and had been adopted by him when a young man and woman had escaped down the Kuukpik (Colville River), having been cut off by a group of Nunamiut.[30] That would place the boy's (Passak) birth between 1842 and 1845. This report may be tied with the battle on the Killik River, but it serves as an indicator of the time period of the displacement along the northern front. Other time line indicators will be addressed later. The Atłiq incident took place during the mid-1820s as a part of the initial attack upon the Koyukon. If so, then the Koyukon were attacked from the north and south simultaneously during the 1820s and lost many warriors during the initial raids against them, including their own raids on Nuvuġaluaq at Point Hope. It was a turning point for the Nuataaġmiut, Kuukpiġmiut, and Nendaaghe Hʉt'aane Koyukon.

Each Kuukpiġmiut regional band in succession ousted the Nendaaghe and Too Loghe Hʉt'aane Koyukon until they were completely defeated and routed from Nendaaghe and northern Too Loghe, their former estates. Their defeat in the upper Kobuk and total abandonment of Nendaaghe and northern Too Loghe took place between approximately 1840 and 1846. This does not mean that all the Koyukon abandoned the area; individual families stayed on for a number of years. Burch reported Iyaġaaġmiut in the Killik River area well into the 1860s.[31] Each Kuukpiġmiut regional band pushed the Koyukon further eastward perhaps in alternate years and/or in successive years. I shall resume the sequence of the Koyukon displacement after addressing the issue of the estate boundaries between Nendaaghe and Too Loghe and delineating the estates of the Di'hąįį Gwich'in and Taghe Chox Xut'ana Lower Tanana, because the subsequent reoccupation of their separate estates can be understood better with this information.

The Koyukon/Koyukon Boundaries

There will never be a way to verify the boundaries between the Nendaaghe and Too Loghe Hʉt'aane Koyukon estates, however, we can extrapolate the possiblities from what we do know. To recapitulate, the Kuukpiġmiut Iñupiat were divided into three regional bands along the Kuukpik (Colville River). Going from up stream to down stream (west to east) they are Kaŋianiġmiut, Killiġmiut, and Qaŋmaliġmiut. Generally each group, in order, exploited the resources around the Itivliim Kuuŋa (Etivluk), Killik, and Anaktuvuk rivers. If there were to be a boundary between the Nendaaghe and Too Loghe estates, the most logical place in terms of habitat exploitation would be along the Killik River. Furthermore, if we travel southward, the Aalaasuk (Alatna River) headwaters, which are within the Too Loghe estate, and the Killik River headwaters are very close and make an easy highway both north and south. If we interject here the comment by Hall that the Killik River appeared "to be a north-south dividing line in terms of house types," then that serves as further evidence of a group boundary. The Nendaaghe Hʉt'aane Koyukon lived in larger permanent communities, whereas the Too Loghe Hʉt'aane Koyukon lived in scattered family groups as Ke'ts'eeggaagge' described them. The Nendaaghe and Too Loghe Hʉt'aane Koyukon were mountain Indians who exploited the Brooks Range both to the north and south on their seasonal rounds, and it appears that the Killik River was their mutual estate boundaries.

The Koyukon/Gwich'in Boundaries

Now to recreate the boundaries between the Too Loghe Hʉt'aane Koyukon and the Di'hąįį Gwich'in to the east. To distinguish between the Too Loghe and Di'haįį estates we can turn to place names; to the oral tradition of the Iñupiat, Koyukon, and Gwich'in; Alexander Hunter Murray's early reports; Robert McDonald's journal; Robert Kennicott's papers;[32] a map drawn by William Lucas Hardisty, the Clerk-in-Charge for the Hudson's Bay Company stationed in Fort Yukon, Alaska from 1852 to 1860;* Jules Jette, Robert McKennan; and Frederick Hadleigh-West (Fig. 20).

The Gwich'in name for Anaktuvuk Pass is K'iitł'it. The people who came from this part of the country were known as K'iitł'it Gwich'in by the the Gwich'in people. It was my initial assumption that the K'iitł'it Gwich'in were a part of the Gwich'in nation,[33] but since then I have drawn the conclusion that the K'iitł'it Gwich'in were the Nendaaghe and Too Loghe Hʉt'aane Koyukon and that K'iitł'it Gwich'in was the Di'haįį Gwich'in ethnonym for them. K'iitł'it was a place name for Anaktuvuk Pass, but it was also the name for the headwaters of the Koyukuk River in general. The Di'haįį Gwich'in name for the John River was K'iitł'uu (Birch Bark Shavings) and the Di'haįį settlement at the mouth of the Eł tseeyh no' (John River) was known as K'iitł'uu. This settlement may be the same settlement known in Koyukon as Neenok'edeleh[34] [place where something (fish) stops (to spawn)].† The Koyukuk River (in Gwich'in) was K'ii, meaning "birch" river. Therefore the name for the Eł tseeyh no' (John River) is K'iitł'uu means "birch bark shavings." These place names are the furthest western place names elicited from the Gwich'in people.[35]

The Koyukon names for the same rivers are; Kkʉyitł'ots'ine for the Koyukuk River meaning "willow at its headwaters" and Eł tseeyh no' for the John River meaning "ochre colored spruce river"[36] ("wind

---

* Hardisty, William Lucas, Biography Sheet, Hudson's Bay Company Archives, Winnipeg, Manitoba, Canada. But according to Murray's reports he arrived in Fort Yukon October 26, 1850, HBCA, B.240/a/4: 13d.

† The place used to be a good seining spot, but its gone now because of re-channeling of the river, *Upper Koyukuk River Place Names*, ANLC Library, author unknown, no date.

Fig. 20. William Lucas Hardisty, Hudson's Bay Company trader stationed in Fort Yukon from 1850–1860. Mr. Hardisty was fluent in Dinjii Zhuh, the language of the Gwich'in. Photo courtesty of Hudson's Bay Company Archives.

river" according to Jette[37]). Another name that was recorded for the John River was Totsenbet[38] which preceded Eł tseeyh no'. How the name Totsenbet (contemporary spelling: Dodzenbeet no'[39]) was elicited is not clear, but it was also a name for a geologic formation in the area.[40] Jette discounted Totsenbet as a Koyukon name for the John River altogether.[41] Too ts'en yee[42] (on the water side[43]) is a mountain at the mouth of the John River. It could be Too ts'en Bede[44] taken from *hᵾbede* (mountain or hill side), hence "mountain or hill side on the water side." Be that as it may, it went out of usage before the turn of the century for when F. C. Schrader went through the country in 1901 he was using John River to describe the K'iitł'uu/Eł tseeyh no'. That the Eł tseeyh no' (John River) had both a Gwich'in and Koyukon name is significant. The eastern most Koyukon ethnonym, recorded by Jette in 1908,[45] is Tlakołnika for either the Middle or North Fork Koyukuk. However, Hʉkkughutne and Hʉkkughutno' have been elicited for the Middle Fork and the North Fork is Tlaakk'ołneekk'e (river through rocky mountains).[46]

Given the linguistic information above, I believe that the Too Loghe Hʉt'aane Koyukon had a shared boundary with the Di'hąįį Gwich'in along the Eł tseeyh no' (John River) and that it extended down the Koyukuk to the Neek'eleh no' (South Fork) at which point the Di'hąįį estate boundary was exhausted. The distribution of the Kavik projectile points, that are associated predominately with the Gwich'in and are found east of the Eł tseeyh no' (John River) and Neek'eleh no' (South Fork), is another compelling reason to establish these rivers as the boundary between the Koyukon and Gwich'in. If we recall K'ets'eeggaagge', the medicine man from the Kateel River, claimed that the upper Koyukuk was occupied by the Donegge kkaa Hʉt'aane (more than one group) and the Too Tleekk'e Hʉt'aane and that both (or all) groups lived in widely scattered family groups. As stated earlier, it is my opinion that Too Tleekk'e Hʉt'aane was actually the Koyukon ethnonym for the Di'hąįį Gwich'in people.

The Di'hąįį Gwich'in

William Lucas Hardisty, a Hudson's Bay Company trader stationed in Fort Yukon, drew a map in 1853 (Fig. 21) with information received from Gwich'in informants. The ethnonyms are all given in Dinjii Zhuh, the language of the Gwich'in people. On the map, the lower Koyukuk is occupied by estate number 10. Tait Sa Koochin (Teets'ii Gwich'in, general Gwich'in ethnonym for the Koyukon) and the upper Koyukuk is occupied by the Keet la Koochin (K'iitł'it Gwich'in). It appears from the map that the K'iitł'it Gwich'in occupied everything above the mouth of the Kk'oonootne (Kanuti River). The map was drawn in 1853 at least two years after the attack at Too Loghe on Olsons Lake. The Di'hąįį Gwich'in do not appear on the map. This was not an over sight. Hardisty was aware of the

Fig. 21. William Lucas Hardisty's map of 1853 with Gwich'in ethnonyms.
Photo courtesy of Hudson's Bay Company Archives.

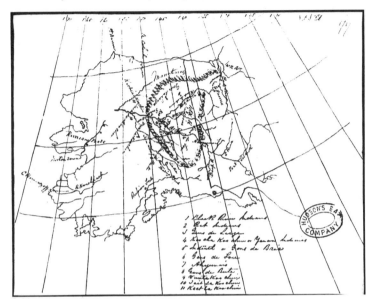

Di'haįį Gwich'in. By 1853, most of the Di'haįį Gwich'in except for
Dits'ii K'iitł'uu at K'iitł'uu (the heart of their former estate) had
vacated the northern and southern areas of their estate.

In 1860–61 Robert Kennicott spent part of the winter in Fort
Yukon, Alaska.[47] There he gathered the following information about
the Di'haįį Gwich'in: "Te ä hin* Kutchin (the country below the
others). Gens de Siffleur. Northwest of the Gens du Large [Neets'aįį
Gwich'in], north to the sea and south to the Youkon River. Formerly
a strong band but now reduced to 4 hunters. They hunt caribou and
in summer subsist to a great extent on siffleurs (marmots or
spermaphiles) whence their name of "Siffleur Indians" given by
whites."[48] This is the only full description of the Di'haįį Gwich'in

---

* The Dinjii Zhuh "d' was often written as "t," and the nasalized vowels "aįį " often
sound as if there is a "n" at the end of the word.

estate that survives. No doubt, this information was passed on by
Hardisty. Hardisty would have known since he was fluent in
Gwich'in,[49] and he visited the area in 1851.[50] This description does
not address the western borders, but it gives us the extent of their
southern borders and range.

To return to the western boundary interface with the Too Loghe
estate we can refer to Robert McDonald (Fig. 22) who visited the
Neets'ąįį Gwich'in in 1867 and spent seven days en route. He
estimated that he had gone 250 miles from Fort Yukon in the process
and said that they were deep in the former Suffleux* (Di'hąįį
Gwich'in) country.[51] Roughly speaking, 250 miles from Fort Yukon
up the Chandalar and down the Koyukuk would place McDonald
along the Tlaakk'ołneekk'e (North Fork), Hʉkkughutno' (Middle
Fork), or the Neek'elehno' (South Fork). Although the Di'hąįį
Gwich'in were already displaced, that would have been consistent

Fig. 22. Robert McDonald. Courtesy of the General Synod Archives,
Toronto.

---

* Misspelling for siffluer.

with K'ets'eeggaagge's 1842 report of two or three groups at the headwaters of the Koyukuk River.

In more recent years the ethnonym for the people of Kk'oonootne[52] (Kanuti River, "well traveled river by both man and animals" or "fish roe river"[53]) has been elicited as Kk'oonootne Hʉt'aane Koyukon.[54] Perhaps this was the other Koyukon group up the Koyukuk River in 1842, but we can not tell for sure. I am inclined to suggest that the Kk'oonoone Hʉt'aane Koyukon was an ethnonym that came along after the 1860s and that up to that time the area was occupied by the Too Loghe Hʉt'aane Koyukon.

Dall made some connections for the upper Koyukuk when he wrote in 1870, "The Koyúkukho-tàna.—These are sendentary Indians living on the Koyúkuk river, and described as Koyúkuns in another part of this volume. They are the Funnakachotana [Yoonegge Hʉt'aane] of Holmberg, and perhaps the Ketlitk-Kutchin [K'iitł'it Gwich'in] of the Hudson Bay voyageurs, who know them only by report. The name means "people of the Koyukuk River."[55] We know that Yoonegge Hʉt'aane means "upland people" and is only a general name for all the residents above the mouth of the Kateel River by the Kodeel Kkaakk'e Hʉt'aane Koyukon who lived about it's confluence with the Koyukuk River. The Too Tleekk'e Hʉt'aane estate and Di'hạịị estates appear to be synonymous.

Given this information, if we return to Too Loghe on Olsons Lake and Alexander, the only survivor who was know to be Gwich'in, we know that Too Loghe was in the Too Tleekk'e Hʉt'aane/Di'hạịị estate. Olsons Lake is at the headwaters of the Kanuti, Ray, and Dall rivers. There are winter trails which connect it to places up the Tlaakk'oɬneekk'e (North Fork) and Neek'elehno' (South Fork) and specifically to K'iitł'uu at the mouth of the Eɬ tseeyh no' (John River). All of this supports McKennan's statement that, "Their territory included the Middle and North forks of the Chandalar River and the headwaters of the Koyukuk River...The Eskimo settlement at 'Little Squaw' on the North Fork of the Chandalar River and at Coldfoot on the Middle Fork of the Koyukuk River is said to be in the heart of territory formerly inhabited by the Dihai Kutchin."[56] Hadleigh-West outlined the same area in 1959.[57] The Di'haįį Gwich'in, like their neighbors to the east and west, were montane people and I doubt if they lived much to the west beyond the mountains on the upper Kk'oonootne (Kanuti River). Besides the upper Kk'oonootne (Kanuti River) was occupied at the time by the Too Loghe Hʉt'aane Koyukon. In 1867 Dall[58] and Whymper[59] both indicate that Newicargut (Nowikákat), at the mouth of the Nowitna River (the Noghee Hʉt'aane Koyukon[60]), was the last Koyukon village before the gathering place at Noochu Logheyet (Nuklúkahyét*). Dall even stated further after a description of the location that "This is Nuklukayet, the neutral ground where all the tribes meet in the spring to trade."[61] The Di'haįį estate and range extended to the Tozitna River just below the confluence of the Tanana and Yukon rivers.

According to Kennicott, the southern borders of the Di'haįį estate were along the Yukon River. If Kennicott heard this from Hardisty, then at some point in time this must have been the case. I think that in 1847 when Alexander Hunter Murray (Fig. 23) established Fort Yukon, the Di'haįį Gwich'in living at Olsons Lake went fishing along the Lower Ramparts between the Ray and Tozitna rivers. At this point Murray was calling the Di'haįį Gwich'in the Lower Indians[†] and distinguished them from the Taghe Chox Xut'ana Lower Tanana whom he called the Middle Band and variously Tchukootchin (people of the water[62]), Tecounka-Kootchin,[63] Teeathaka,[64] Tchuktchis, and Tchutakchis.[65] Murray said they numbered twenty men.[66] The Taghe Chox Xut'ana Lower Tanana occupied the Yukon River from the Dall River to Birch Creek. I think that the Yukon River between

---

* Nuclukayette, at the time, was not a community or post. Raymond in 1869 identified it as, "At the mouth of the Tanana is the trading ground called Nuclucayette, where the Indians inhabiting the banks of this tributary are accustomed to congregate in the spring." 1871: 23.

† Murray used "the Lower Indians" in reference to the lower band of the Gwichyaa Gwich'in led by Shahnyaati' (Deenduu Gwich'in), the Di'haįį Gwich'in in the Lower Ramparts, and the Noghee Hʉt'aane Koyukon living at Nowikáket (Newicargut).

Fig. 23. Alexander Hunter Murray and his wife taken after his retirement.
Photo courtesy of Hudson's Bay Company Archives.

Ray River and the Tozitna River was within the Di'haii estate and
range and that they occupied it year around.

There are several clues which support the idea of the Di'haii
Gwich'in presence along the Lower Ramparts of the Yukon River.
The first of these is Murray who, on November 4, 1848, reports
"Kooceatii, a leader of the lower band arrived with twelve of his
followers." This same Kooceatii (G) is mentioned several times as
Kooceatii, Kooeeante,[67] Koongahte,[68] and Kooeeawtee[69]—all
variants of the same Gwich'in name. The current spelling is
Gook'aahtii.[70] Gook'aahtii was the oldest son of Dits'ii K'iitł'uu,[71]

---

* Khaihkwaii was the name for the community leader before the title of chief was
introduced among the Gwich'in. Kkuskkaa has a similar meaning (community leader)
in Koyukon and is a very old word. In Lower Tanana, *tyone* is equivalent to the Koyukon
Doyon: a big areawide political leader.

Fig. 24. Dall's Vocabulary lists for Tenán Kutchin 1867.

Of the 142 words in his vocabulary 44 of them were Gwich'in words, 18 were Gwich'in stems combined with "other" language prefixes and suffixes.

Gwich'in words 44

18 Gwich'in stems 18

Total Gwich'in influence 62

Total Tenán Kutchin words 142

43% of the Tenán Kutchin words are Gwich'in words.

Examples:

English	Tenán Kutchin	Lower Tanana	Contemporary Gwich'in
pipe	sitedchi	ts'adetthee'	ts'eet'itchi'
water	chū	too	chuu
aurora	yukhói	yoyekoyh	yakạih, yakaih
blood	tahnéh	del	dah
you	nun	nenh	nan, nanh
we, ours*	nohún	nuxunh, xunh	nakhwan
winter	hwoi	xuyh	khaii
brown bear	sih	tsonee	shih
black bear	sūs	sresr	shoh
woman	trinjóh	tr'axa	tr'injaa, tr'injoo†
river	húneh	hun'a	han

None of the kinship terms were in the Gwich'in language.

* Probably "you pl.," but misplaced in order. All the words mean you "pl."

† Older form of word.

the Di'hąįį Gwich'in *khaihkwaii*[*] at K'iitł'uu at the mouth of Eł tseeyh no' (John River). Gook'ąąhtii Khaihkwaii did not have any children,[72] consequently his name had two meanings: "he took care of them" and "the uncle who watched over them." It is far from clear whether Gook'ąąhtii was a real or adopted son of Dits'ii K'iitł'uu. Dits'ii K'iitł'uu khaihkwaii adopted many women and children; only his younger children and those who survived the unknown illness in 1847–48[73] and the scarlet fever epidemic of 1865 are accounted for. Gook'ąąhtii Khaihkwaii was living along the Lower Yukon Ramparts from Ray River to the Tozitna River year round. The important point is that Gook'ąąhtii Khaihkwaii was a Di'hąįį Gwich'in *khaihkwaii* who was living along the Yukon River along the Lower Yukon Ramparts year a round in 1848.

At the rapids was a community called Kuhel li'[74] named by McKennan's informant Joe Number 6 who said that Shahnyaati' (referred to as Young Chief and Little Chief by Murray[75]), the well known Gwichyaa Gwich'in *khaihkwaii*, originally came from that location. Joe Number 6 offered no translation for the word, but Hadleigh-West offered Kwohelin,[76] suggesting that the ancestors of the Neets'ąįį Gwich'in came from this area and that the word might mean "secrets disappearing." This could not be, since no such word exists in Dinjii Zhuh. Perhaps it was Hadleigh-West's informants' only way to communicate that this knowledge was disappearing. I will cover the Neets'ąįį Gwich'in with their Tanana River connections and the McKennan confusion with the phratries later. In either case, it seems that the informants were making an effort to pronounce a word in another language. Peter John (b. 1900) of Minto, Alaska stated that he heard there was a community above the rapids called Xulenh Kayeh, which was occupied by a mixture of people— Gwich'in, Lower Tanana, and Koyukon—at one time.[77] Whymper, on his 1868 map, shows the Lower Ramparts occupied by the "Nuclukayette Indianer"[78] (Fig. 2, page 6). There is solid evidence for the accuracy of this oral account based on the vocabularies collected by Dall[79] (Fig. 24) Dall Vocabularies 1867). Fully forty-

three percent of the Tenán Kutchin vocabulary is influenced by
Gwich'in words. The "Tannin-Kootchin" are the Lower Tanana of
the Minto Flats; they appear as "9. Vunta Koo chin" (those who
dwell among the lakes) on Hardisty's map (Fig. 25). They are also
referred to as Tenán Kutchin,[80] Benh Te Hʉt'aane, and Tenen
Hʉt'aane[81] (Koyukon ethnonym for them.) Their ethnonym for
themselves is Menhtee Xu'tana. Shahnyaati' Khaihwaii was at a fish
camp site on the north side of the Yukon just below the rapids. It
was the first community encountered by Raymond in 1869 during
his descent of the Yukon River and was noted on his map as Senati
Village.[82] If Shahnyaati' did come from Xulenh kayeh originally,
then that might account for the name of his youth: Que-eech-et[83]
(Gwi'eech'it, gwi'ee, "coming this way," "bringing this way toward
speaker," and ch'it, older version of "the first" or "coming this way
first," the implication being that others came later.) However,
Shahnyaati's father, Dahjalti' Khaihkwaii, was a Neets'ąįį Gwich'in[84]
person. This would imply that Shahnyaati' moved from the Neets'ąįį
to the Deenduu estate earlier in his life. He undoubtedly had close
family connections with other community leaders through marriage.
It seems that Shahnyaati' lived along the Lower Ramparts on a
seasonal basis for fishing, but his primary residence was in the
vicinity of Birch Creek[85] and, as stated earlier, he was a Deenduu
Gwich'in khaihkwaii. It would be fair to say that Shahnyaati'
Khaihkwaii and Gook'ąąhtii Khaihkwaii knew each other, were
probably related (distantly or through marriage), and occasionally
lived and traveled together. It was McKennan's questioning about
Shahnyaati' that brought out the name of the community which has
been interfaced with Peter John's Xulenh Kayeh in the Lower
Ramparts. Although it was named Senati Village by Raymond, it
probably was nothing more than the place where Shahnyaati' was
fishing for that particular summer of 1869.

There is reason to believe that at least a few of the place names
in the area of the Lower Ramparts went through a language transition.
In 1848, the mountains to the west and south of the Yukon River

Fig. 25. Koyukon, Gwich'in, and Lower Tanana Estates, 1846. Map created by Karen Ferrall and Adeline Raboff.

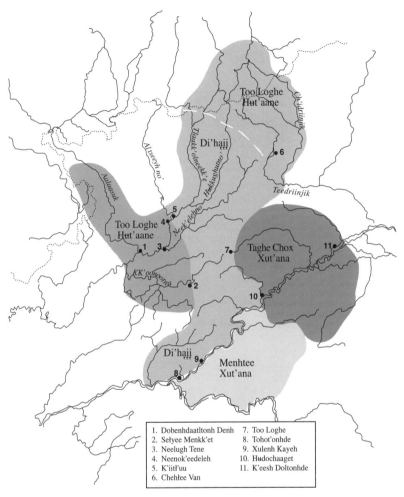

1. Dobenhdaatltonh Denh
2. Seɫyee Menkk'et
3. Neelugh Tene
4. Neenok'eedeleh
5. K'iitl'uu
6. Chehɫee Van
7. Too Loghe
8. Tohot'onhde
9. Xulenh Kayeh
10. Hᵾdochaaget
11. K'eesh Doltonhde

were known as the Big Beaver[86] [Tsee Choo (G)] Mountains, somewhere in the interim that range of mountains has lost the name completely. The earliest recorded name for Ray River was Chetaut River.[87] The original name, Chetaut, could be translated as Ch'itaa (over the top, going over the top) or Ch'itaa'at (the wife of going over the top) in Gwich'in. The Koyukon name for the same river is Tseet'o no' (literally beneath Tsee River, beneath Cache River, or beneath Beaver River.)[88] Tsii or Tsee meaning "cache" or "beaver" in Gwich'in with a Koyukon -no' added for river. This shows a transition[89] from an original Gwich'in name to the Koyukon, Tseet'o no', which is the adaptation and incorporation of a basic Gwich'in name into Koyukon. Typically the Koyukon substituted their name for creek -no' for -njik which is the Gwich'in equivalent. This demonstrates that the Ray River was formerly occupied by Gwich'in speakers and that the Koyukon speakers came later. Presently, from the Dall River to Birch Creek there are ten names which are of Koyukon or Lower Tanana origin. According to Kari, "This suggests that all the names reported by Raymond in the district were from Koyukon speakers, and that as early as 1869 Koyukonized versions of Gwich'in place names were being used."[90]

For all the above reasons I think that the Di'haii Gwich'in occupied the Yukon River from the Tseet'o no' (Ray River) to the Tozitna River. To review, they are (1) Hardisty's map of 1853, (2) Kennicott's description of the Di'haii Gwich'in estate, (3) the discovery that the Too Tleekk'e Hut'aane and the Di'haii Gwich'in are the same people, (4) Murray's 1848 labeling of the Di'haii Gwich'in as the Lower Band and the Taghe Chox Xut'ana Lower Tanana as the Middle Band, (5) the naming of Gook'aahtii Khaihkwaii in 1848 and placing him along the Yukon River, (6) the discovery of Xulenh kayeh, the mixed Koyukon, Lower Tanana, and Gwich'in community in the Lower Ramparts, (7) Dall's vocabulary list for the Tenán Kutchin which supports the oral accounts, and (8) the transition from Gwich'in to Koyukon names in the area of the ramparts. These, I believe, are evidence of the southern boundaries of the Di'haii Gwich'in in the Lower Ramparts.

Now to continue with the Di'haii Gwich'in northeastern interface with the Neets'aii Gwich'in, again Kennicott, "Northwest of the Gens du Large [Neets'aii Gwich'in], north to the sea," and Hadleigh-West, "It was further stated that the middle fork [Ch'idriinjik[91]] of the

Chandalar and the Chandalar proper to some little distance below
the present village of Venetie were also within their country."[92]
Ch'idriinjik (Middle Fork, Chandalar River) is northwest of the
Neets'ạįį estate and there is a pass that goes to the north slope (of
the Brooks Range) from there to the Sagavanirktok River. According
to Simpson's map (Fig. 5, page 19) the "Mountainous Indians"
occupy the mountains, however this is only a general overview. The
Di'hạįį estate occupied the upper Itkillik and Sagavanirktok rivers.
Basically that was the Di'hạįį estate in the 1840s.

Taghe Chox Xut'ana Lower Tanana

The Taghe Chox Xut'ana Lower Tanana estate as defined earlier
is from the Dall River to the Lower Birch Creek along the Yukon
River. Their estate begins at the lower mouth of the Birch Creek*
and includes all the numerous drainages in between, but mainly the
Hadweendzik Creek (Heegwinjik or Oozriinjik[93]) and Beaver Creek.†
Their estate also included the mountains to the north and south (Tsee
Choo Mountains) of these drainages. As their name says, they were
a Lower Tanana group. Murray said, "The Middle Band and the
People of the Butes speak the same." This means that they spoke the
Lower Tanana language, but since they had Gwich'in neighbors both
up the river and in the Lower Ramparts, they probably spoke a
combination, a Lower Tanana framework with borrowed Gwich'in
words and stems. The late Leonard John, of Stevens Village, Alaska
said that "Once there were some people who lived around here that
spoke a different language from our language now [Koyukon]."[94]
This coincides very well with Hardisty's group, "5. Indǐuth or Gens
de Bris," in figure 28. It also corresponds with the "Ttyoni" in
McDonald's journal entry of June 1864, October 1865, March 1866,

---

* K'ii Dootin Njik (Standing Birch Creek) in Gwich'in. Matthews, et. al., 1999: 83,
K'eesh Doltonh No' in Koyukon.

† Tsonjege, Tsonjek, Tso gho Neek'e in Koyukon, Matthews et. al., 1999: 81. Tseenjik
in Gwich'in.

and February 1867.[95] Katherine Arndt postulated that this may be the same group as the Gens de Millieu (middle people).[96] The word "ttyoni" also appears as "tyone" by Lieutenant Henry T. Allen in 1885 who used it thus, "We heard much of Nicolai, the proprietor of Taral, Tyone* of Chittyna, and chief trader among the natives..."[97] The Taghe Chox Xut'ana Lower Tanana were an intermediate group of Lower Tanana speakers who were between the Di'haįį and Deenduu estates on the Yukon River in 1848.

Having established the estates of the Too Loghe Hʉt'aane Koyukon, Di'haįį Gwich'in, and Taghe Chox Xut'ana Lower Tanana in 1848, we can now turn our attention to the Nendaaghe and Too Loghe Hʉt'aane Koyukon displacement in the area of Anaktuvuk Pass. This time we will include the Koyukon perspective and specific genealogies that connect the people from Venetie, Arctic Village, Birch Creek, Stevens Village, and Allakaket to the Nendaaghe and Too Loghe Hʉt'aane Koyukon and the displacement of the Di'haįį Gwich'in and Taghe Chox Xut'ana Lower Tanana. The movement of all four groups took place very rapidly. The Nendaaghe and Too Loghe Hʉt'aane Koyukon vacated their estates by 1846-47, the Di'haįį Gwich'in by 1855, and the Taghe Chox Xut'ana Lower Tanana just barely survived through a few individuals.

---

* Lower Tanana *tyone* equivalent to *doyon* in Koyukon.

PART 3, CHAPTER NOTES

1. Helge Ingstad, *Nunamiut*, (New York: W. W. Norton & Company, 1954: 128; Nicholas J. Gubser, *"Comparative Study of the Intellectual Culture of the Nunamiut Eskimos at Anaktuvuk Pass, Alaska,"* (Fairbanks: University of Alaska, 1961: 84; Grant Spearman, Joshua Rulland, personal communication, 1999.

2. Rachael Riley, personal communication, 1999.

3. Richard E. Morlan, "The Later Prehistory of the Middle Porcupine Drainage, Northern Yukon Territory," Mercury Series, Archaeological Survey of Canada, Paper No. 11, National Museum of Canada, Ottowa, 1973: ii– iii.

4. Ibid.: 477.

5. Mike Kunz, personal communication, 1999.

6. John M. Campbell, "Cultural Succession at Anaktuvuk Pass, Arctic Alaska," Arctic Institute of North America, Technical Paper No. 11, Montreal, 1962: 39–54.

7. John M. Campbell, "The Kavik site of Anaktuvuk Pass, Central Brooks Range Alaska," *Anthropological papers of the University of Alaska* 14, no. 1 (1968): 32–42.

8. Ibid.

9. Morlan (1973): 480.

10. Herbert L. Alexander, *Putu: A Fluted Point Site In Alaska*, Department of Archaeology Simon Fraser University, Publication No. 17 (Burnaby, B.C.: 1987):39.

11. Donald W. Clark, personal communication, 1999.

12. Herbert L. Alexander, *"Prehistory of the Central Brooks Range, An Archaeological Analysis,"* (Ph.D. diss., University of Oregon, University of Alaska microfilm, Ann Arbor, 1969): 26.

13. Edwin S. Hall, Jr., "Speculation on the Late Prehistory of the Kutchin Athapaskans," *Ethnohistory* 16, no. 4 (1969): 317–333.

14. Ibid.: 326.

15. Jules Jette, Sr., notes on Koyukon place names, 1908a, microfilm AL17: 426a–537, JOPA, Foley Library, Gonzaga University, Spokane, Washington, 115 pp.

16. Moses Johnson, et. al., *"Allakaket-Alatna Area Native Placenames,"* comp. Eliza Jones with contributions by Wendy Arundale, ms., October 1997: 11.

17. *Upper Koyukuk River Place Names*, No. 28 (Fairbanks: Alaska Native Language Center Library, University of Alaska Fairbanks, n.d.): 160; Jones and Arundale (1997): 25.

18. John P. Cook, personal communication, 1999.

19. Edwin S. Hall, Jr., "An Archaeological Survey of Interior Northwest Alaska," *Anthropological Papers of the University of Alaska* 17, no. 2 (1975): 19.

20. Hall (1970): 11.

21. Edwin S. Hall, Jr., "A Preliminary Analysis of House Types at Tukuto Lake, Northern Alaska," *The Interior Peoples of Northern Alaska*, ed. Edwin S. Hall, Jr., Archaeological Survey of Canada Paper No. 49, Ottawa, National Museum of Man, 1976: 98.

22. Rachel Riley, personal communication, 1999.

23. Simon Paneak, tape 842, transcript, University of New Mexico, Center for Southwest Research, September 1971: 1–3.

24. Justus Mekiana, Killik River Data, tape 11:6, trans. Grant Spearman, 4 May 1990.

25. Burch (1998b): 117.

26. Simon Paneak, tape 842, transcript, 1971.

27. William Irving, field notes with Simon Paneak, 1950, personal communication with Ernest S. Burch, Jr., 17 April 1980.

28. Paneak, tape 842, 1971: 1–3.

29. Ernest S. Burch, Jr., and Craig W. Mishler, "The Di'haii Gwich'in: Mystery People of Northern Alaska," *Arctic Anthropology* 32, no. 1 (1995), 153.

30. Maguire (1988): 410.

31. Burch (1998b): 117.

32. Robert Kennicott, Manuscript No. 203-b, U. S. National Anthropological Archives, Smithsonian Institution, Washington, D. C., 1962.

33. Adeline Peter Raboff, "Preliminary Study of the Western Gwich'in Bands," *American Indian Culture and Research Journal* 23, no. 2 (1999): 1–25.

34. *Upper Koyukuk River Place Names* (Fairbanks: Alaska Native Language Center Library, University of Alaska Fairbanks, n.d.); Jones and Arundale (1997): 9. I have chosen the latest spelling.

35. Steven Tsee Gho', Tsyaa Tsal Peter, Sr., personal communication, 1987–97. This reference will be shortened to STP, 1987–97 throughout this text.

36. *Upper Koyukuk River Place Names* (n.d.)

37. Jules Jette, Alaska Native Language Center Library, University of Alaska, 1910.

38. Walter C. Mendenhall, *Reconnaisance from Fort Hamlin to Kotzebue Sound, Alaska by way of Dall, Kanuti, Allen, Kowak Rivers*, 1902:19, 39, map between pages 20–21.

39. James M. Kari, personal communication, 1999.

40. Mendenhall, 1902.

41. Jette, 1910.

42. Eliza Jones, personal communication, 1999.

43. James Kari, personal communication, 1999.

44. Ibid.

45. Jules Jette, notes on Koyukuk placenames, 1908a.

46. Jones and Arundale (1997): item 171:11.

47. Morgan B. Sherwood, *Exploration of Alaska 1865–1900* (Fairbanks: University of Alaska Press, 1992): 17.

48. Kennicott (1862).

49. Letter dated 16 November 1851, HBCA d.5/32: 236–37.

50. HBCA, B.240/a/4, fo. 19.

51. "Recent Intelligence," *Church Missionary Record* XIII, no. 10 (October 1868): 289.

52. Moses Henzie, *Moses Henzie*, Yukon-Koyukuk School District Series, (Vancouver, B. C.: Hancock House Publishers Ltd., 1979): 14.

53. Alaska Native Language Center Library (n.d.); Jones and Arundale (1997): 12.

54. Jette and Jones, Koyukon Athabascan Dictionary, ms.

55. William H. Dall, *Alaska and Its Resources*, 2nd ed. (Arno & The New York Times, 1970): 431.

56. Robert McKennan, *The Chandalar Kutchin*, Arctic Institute of North America Technical Paper No. 17 (New York, 1965): 23.

57. Frederick Hadleigh-West, "On the Distribution and Territory of the Western Kutchin Tribes," *Anthropology Papers of the University of Alaska* 7, no. 2 (College, Alaska: May 1959): 114.

58. Dall (1970): 53.

59. Frederick Whymper, *Travel and Adventure in the Territory of Alaska*, 2nd ed. (Readex Microprint Corporation, 1966): 199, 210.

60. Jette and Jones, Koyukon Athabascan Dictionary, ms.

61. Dall (1970): 93.

62. Alexander Hunter Murray, *Journal of the Yukon 1847–48*, (Ottowa: Government Printing Bureau, 1910): 84.

63. Ibid.: 81.

64. Ibid.

65. Ibid.: 84.

66. Ibid.: 81.

67. Murray, journal entry for 14 June 1951, B.240/a/5.

68. Hudson's Bay Company Archives, B.240/a/8.

69. HBCA, B.240/a/4.

70. Katherine Peter, personal communication, 1998.

71. STP, 1987–97.

72. Ibid.

73. HBCA, B.240/a/1, B.240/a/2.

74. Robert McKennan, notes, University of Alaska Archives.

75. Murray (1910): 68, 88.

76. Hadleigh-West, "The Netsi Kutchin: An Essay in Human Ecology," (Ph. D. diss. in Anthropology, Louisiana State University and Agricultural and Mechanical College, Baton Rouge, Louisiana, 1963): 228.

77. Peter John (1999).

78. Whymper (1966): inside cover.

79. Dall (1970): 566–575.

80. Ibid.: 566.

81. Jette and Jones, Koyukon Athabascan Dictionary, ms.

82. Captain Charles W. Raymond, *Report of a Reconnaissance of the Yukon River, Alaska Territory, July to September, 1869* (Washington: Government Press Office, 1871): 22.

83. Strachan Jones, "The Kutchin Tribes," notes on the Tenneh or Chepewyan Indians of British and Russian America, Annual Report, Smithsonian Institute, 1866: 320–327.

84. STP, Dahjalti' vizheh k'aa, 1987–97.

85. Dall (1970): 101, 102; William Schneider, *Beaver, Alaska: The Story of a Multi-Ethnic Community*, paper submitted to the faculty of Bryn Mawr College, 1976: 315–326.

86. Murray (1910): 77; Whymper (1966): inside jacket cover. Hudson Stuck, *Ten Thousand Miles with a Dog Sled*, 2nd ed., (Prescott, Arizona: Wolfe Publishing Co., Inc., 1988): 343. Beaver Mountains.

87. Raymond (1871): 21 and Appendix D, Table of Distances on the Yukon River.

88. Margaret Matthews, et.al., "Stevens Village Land Use Plan, Ethnogeography of Ancestral Lands and Integrated Resources Management Plan," (Stevens Village, Alaska: Stevens Village Council, 1999): 66.

89. Ibid.: 83.

90. Matthews, et. al. (1999): 83.

91. Richard A. Caulfield and Walter Peter, Subsistence Division, Alaska Department of Fish and Game, U. S. Geological Survey 250,000 series Maps, 1982: item 29.

92. Hadleigh-West (1959): 113.

93. Caulfield, et. al. (1982): Item #128.

94. Leonard John, "How Stevens Village Came to Be," *Alaska Sportsman*, August (1959): pp 32–34.

95. McDonald, journal, 1910.

96. Arndt (1996): 205.

97. Henry T. Allen, *An Expedition to The Copper, Tanana and Koyukuk Rivers 1885* (Anchorage, Alaska: Alaska Northwest Publishing Co.): 45.

Oolah Pass, Brooks Range

Photograph by Dennis Witmer

Kurupa Lake, looking south

Photograph by Dennis Witmer

Kurupa Lake, looking west

Photograph by Dennis Witmer

South of Kurupa Lake, looking south

Photograph by Dennis Witmer

Kurupa Lake, looking southeast

Photograph by Dennis Witmer

Early Snowfall, EAST OF KURUPA LAKE

PHOTOGRAPH BY DENNIS WITMER

Anaktuvuk River: Rock blind, looking east, east of Anaktuvuk Pass

Photograph by Dennis Witmer

HORACE MOUNTAIN, 1899

Photograph by F.C. Schrader, 1899. Courtesy of U.S.G.S.

PART IV

THE FINAL BATTLE AT ANAKTUVUK PASS

THE FINAL BATTLE AT ANAKTUVUK PASS

After years of mutual antagonism, the Nendaaghe Hʉt'aane Koyukon were displaced from their estate between 1840 and 1844 by the Nuataaġmiut and Kuukpiġmiut Iñupiat. First in the upper Nunataaq (Noatak River) and then in the Howard Pass area. The battle at Killik River, where the Uyaġaaġmiut lost twenty men and the Killiġmiut lost four women and two men, was fought at the boundary between the Nendaaghe and Too Loghe estates. The final showdown at K'iitł'it (Anaktuvuk Pass) took place just north of Tulugaq Lake. Once again, Panniaq:

> In other words, according to story, way before [the present] Nunamiut [inland Iñupiat] fight Indians [Nendaaghe and Too Loghe Hʉt'aane Koyukon], away from here,…they had to fight and big fights as I call it at the mouth of (Itikmaliayuk Creek) about five miles north of Tulugaq [Lake], somehow these old Eskimo [Qaŋmaliġmiut regional band] are too smart…Among the Indian [Nendaaghe and Too Loghe Hʉt'aane Koyukon and Di'hạịị Gwich'in] lose over 20 or more…A lot of them, never mentioned how many cause there is no time to count them, shortly after the fighting then Indian [Nendaaghe and Too Loghe Hʉt'aane Koyukon and Di'hạịị Gwich'in] never bothered from that time on the northern slope and afterwards they learn the Indian [Uyaġaaġmiut] move over to the Chandalar area, no Eskimo can follow them.…[1]

Here Panniaq summed up the final battle and tells us that the Uyaġaaġmiut went to the Chandalar River area. According to Ingstad,

from forty to sixty Indians were killed.[2] The aftermath of this battle
can be summed up best by Gubser, "Later, the following spring, the
Nunamiut encountered the Indians [along the Killik River[3]] and saw
that they looked pretty weak and thin."[4] In another place Panniaq
says that all the Uyaġaaġmiut men came back and tried to attack the
Iñupiat several times, but they did not succeed. Finally one spring
the Kuukpiġmiut Iñupiat found the Uyaġaaġmiut along the Killik
River exhausted and starving. At this point the Iñupiat gave them an
ultimatum. They were tired of killing each other and they pointed
out they could easily kill them right there, but instead they asked
them to leave the country and not to come back.[5] Gubser follows
up, "The Nunamiut did not take the offensive...That summer the
Indians travelled to the east along the [north] front of the mountain
line of the Brooks Range and crossed by way of the Itkillik or other
nearby valley to the southeastern Brooks Range, the Chandalar Lake
country, and joined the Indians living there who spoke and lived
like themselves."[6]

The Uyaġaaġmiut "joined the Indians living there [Cheh≯ee Van
(Chandalar Lake)] who spoke and lived like themselves." Who were
the people living at Chandalar Lake in the 1840s? We know that
Cheh≯ee Van (Chandalar Lake) is within the Di'hąįį estate and that
Kennicott stated in 1860:61 that there were four hunters left among
them. In 1867 K'iit≯'it Gwich'in (Nendaaghe and Too Loghe Hʉt'aane
Koyukon) were living within the Di'hąįį estate. We know that Mary
Ch'iyikgwaddhah* told her daughter-in-law, Soozun Peter, that she
grew up there as a young child.[7] Mary was a K'iit≯'it Gwich'in and
even one of her other names confirms this, Vits'ii K'iit≯'it[8] (her
grandfather is from K'iit≯'it). Mary was born approximately 1844.[9]
That means she could have grown up around Chandalar Lake during
the 1840s and later. If this was the case, then the Nendaaghe and

---

* Herbert, Belle, *Shandaa: In My Lifetime*, edited by Bill Pfisterer and Jane McGary,
Alaska Native Language Center, 1988: 82. This particular Ch'iyikgwaddah not to be
confused with Ch'ighik Gwadhaa in Belle Herbert's book. *Shandaa* means "my life in
the presence of my being."

Too Loghe Hʉt'aane Koyukon had either joined the Di'haįį Gwich'in through intermarriage as refugees or agressively as antagonists. I think that all of those conditions prevailed. During the areawide famine of 1849–50, Murray reported that in March 1850[10] the Neets'aįį and Vantee (or Dagǫǫ) Gwich'in were reduced to eleven men and nine boys. This, coupled with the scarlet fever epidemic of 1865, caused the Porcupine and Yukon rivers to be depopulated[11] of all but a few of their original members, this allowed the Nendaaghe and Too Loghe Hʉt'aane Koyukon to move into these areas unhindered. There is only one way to account for the repopulation of the Neets'aįį estate: immigration. Panniaq was right, the Koyukon joined other members of the Koyukon at Chandalar Lake, but who was to have known that except those who knew?

According to McDonald, the K'iitł'it Gwich'in (Koyukon) numbered 180: 40 men, 40 women, and 100 children in 1867.[12] It was after the 1845-46 defeat at K"iitł'it (Anaktuvuk Pass) that the Nendaaghe and Too Loghe Hʉt'aane Koyukon moved to Chehłee Van (Chandalar Lake). I believe they moved there one group at a time. As early as 1865 McDonald reported Yukon drainage Indians (Neets'aįį, Vuntet, and Dagǫǫ Gwich'in) working for the Hudson's Bay Company on the Peel and McKenzie rivers. They packed supplied over the portage between Fort McPherson* and LaPierre's House on the upper Porcupine River and some of them stayed on in the area. By 1867 McDonald counted seventy-six Neets'aįį Gwich'in, which means that between 1850 and 1867 the Di'haįį Gwich'in (and Nendaaghe and Too Loghe Hʉt'aane Koyukon) had already moved onto the Neets'aįį estate and further eastward. Meanwhile let us examine the Hudson's Bay Company Debtors Sheet for 1851 and 1855—the only years that there were separate debtors sheets at the archives.

The Hudson's Bay Company in Fort Yukon had a list of debtors and on those rosters are names of Nendaaghe and Too Loghe

* Along the upper Peel River.

Fig. 26. Too Loghe Hʉt'aane Koyukon and Di'ḥaii Gwich'in origin names

---

Hudson's Bay Archives Debtors Sheets.

1851

Beetsekyetla* (Vits'ii K'iitła)
His grandfather is from K'iitła, K'iitł'it, K'iitł'uu

Kooeeawtee (Gook'a̱a̱htii)
The uncle who watches over them

Neeveete' (Neeveeti', Neeveetii)
The father or uncle of Neevee†

Etcheontah (‡Itj'i'oonta', Ch'ij'i'oonta')
He is holding an animal's antlers.

1855

Beetsekyetla (Vits'ii K'iitła)

Tetseeooze (Teets'iioozhii, Dits'iioozhii)§
He has a Koyukon name
He's named after his grandfather

Echeoontah (Iji'oonta',Ch'ij'i'oonta)

Titseatso (Teets'iiats'oo, Dits'iiats'oo)
A Koyukon with fair complexion
His grandfather was fair of complexion

Betesarathun (Vats'ach'arathan)
We leave things to his discretion

Koongahte (Gook'a̱a̱htii)

Tekeetla (Tiik'iitła, Teek'iitła)
His uncle is from the headwaters of the Koyukuk River
He lives among the K'iitł'it Gwich'in

Tetseeashe (Dits'iioazhii, Dits'iiashii, Teets'iioazhii, Teets'iiashii)
He is named after his grandfather
He comforts and amuses his grandfather
He has a Koyukon name
He reigns upon the Koyukon

Checheenjo [Ch'ijiinjaa, (John)]

Tetsekeetlit [Teets'iik'iitł'it Dits'iik'iitł'it (death outfit)]
Koyukon from the headwaters of the Koyukuk River
His grandfather came from K'iitł'it
This could be the Di'ḥaii patriarch Dits'ii K'iitł'uu

---

* From 'b' in Koyukon and Lower Tanana to 'v' in Gwich'in
† Could be a more general Gwich'in name
‡ Older form
§ The 't' often pronounced as 'd'

Hʉt'aane Koyukon and Di'hąįį Gwich'in origin (Fig. 26). This list, in itself, does not indicate where these people were from. However, it's their names and what they mean that points to known Nendaaghe and Too Loghe Hʉt'aane Koyukon and Di'hąįį Gwich'in people. Take, for instance, Etcheontah who appears on both the 1851 and 1855 list; that is Ch'ij'i'oonta' (he is holding an animal's antlers.) Ch'ij'i'oonta' was originally a member of the Nendaaghe or Too Loghe Hʉt'aane Koyukon or K'iitł'it Gwich'in. Ch'ichi'i'oonta' was his Di'hąįį Gwich'in name; his Koyukon name has been lost. He was the father of Mary Ch'iyikgwaddhah (Figs. 27, 28) and by way of association resided at Chehłee Van (Chandalar Lake) during the 1840s. Later he may have spent time at K'ahtsik,* at the mouth of the Teedriinjik (Chandalar River), and eventually settled along the Draanjik (Black River) with other Nendaaghe and Too Loghe

Fig. 27. Robert, Horace, Jean Virginia, unknown child, Laura, Mary, and Margaret John. 1899. Photo courtesy of USGS.

---

* Margaret Kelly, personal communication, Fort Yukon, Alaska, May, 1994. "It's supposed to be *ahtsik*, but they call it *k'ahtsik*." Ahtsik is the fish basket that is a part of the fish trap, which with all its' parts is called *daa'anlee*.

Fig. 28. Jean Virginia John (later Flitt), unknown child, Laura, Mary, and Margaret John taken by Frank Schrader near Horace Mountain and Phoebe Creek up the head of the Hʉkkughutno' (Middle Fork Koyukuk River), 1899. Photo courtesy of USGS.

Fig. 29. Peter Dinjii Ts'ik Shajool (John) and his granddaughters Myra Henry Peter Francis and Joan Peter. Photo courtesy of Robert McKennan Collection, Dartmouth University.

Fig. 30. Margaret and Ellen John, the daughters of John Deeghozhraii and Mary Ch'antsihch'ok. Margaret was the mother of the late Stephen Fredson. Photograph taken in Fort Yukon, Alaska, c. 1904. Courtesy of the Raboff Collection.

Hʉt'aane Koyukon (K'iitł'it Gwich'in) who had also spent a number of years in the Di'hąįį and/or Neets'ąįį estates[13] (Fig. 31). His son and Mary Ch'iyikgwaddhah's younger brother, William Ross (b. circa 1859), were on the 1900 census for the Black River area. Among the others up the Draanjik (Black River) were Salmon Choo, the nephew of Làrryil[*] (also known as Deech'i' Choo, "big old man"[14]) and Tee oshiiti',[†] the father of John Gwat'an[15] Cruikshank (b. 1865[16]) (Fig. 32). In 1847, Murray said that the Neets'ąįį Gwich'in numbered forty men,[17] with their wives and children that could have been a

---

* Raboff, 1999: 12. Written incorrectly as Ralyil. The "r" is rolled in this name. According to Katherine Peter, Làrryil had many names. This particular name may have had French origins since McDonald's entry for 12/11/1865 talks of "L'original sometimes chief." He would have been a *khaihkwaii*, because he had a caribou fence. The rolled "r" is more common in French loan words among the Eastern Gwich'in.

† STP, 1987–97. This is probably McDonald's *Tevisinti*, Journal entry 3/28/1864. He may have been another one of Shahnyaati's brothers. Shahnyaati's father, Dahjalti', had five wives and many adopted children. Shahnyaati' adopted and raised John Gwat'an, the son of Tee oshiiti'.

Fig. 31. Ch'iji'oonta' Vizhee K'aa Family Tree.

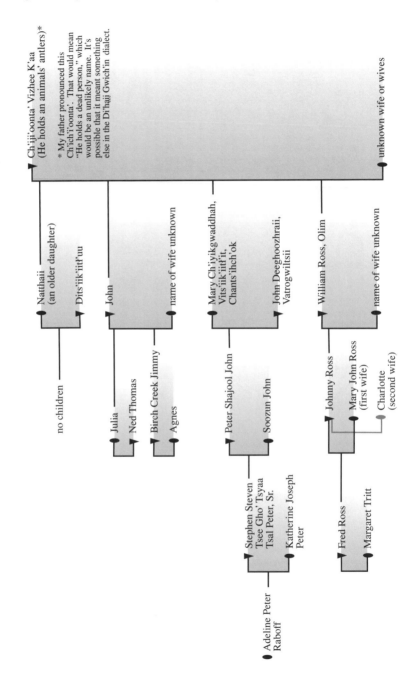

Fig. 32. John Gwatan Chruikshank and his wife Alice (seated) and their children Sophie Paul, Moses Chruikshank, and Charlotte Adams. Date unknown. Courtesy of the Mary Nathanial Collection.

total population of 200; in 1850 there were eleven men and nine boys left from the Neets'ạiị and Vantee Gwich'in; and in December 1865 McDonald said that they lost twenty-seven more people. McDonald counted seventy-six people on his 1867 trip to the Neets'ạiị Gwich'in.[18] It appears that Chehłee Van (Chandalar Lake) Koyukon moved down after the 1865 scarlet fever epidemic which depopulated the Taghe Chox Xut'ana Lower Tanana, the Neets'ạiị, Gwichyaa, and Draanjik Gwich'in, the people along the Yukon above the Lower Ramparts, and the Black River country up the Porcupine River. A few of the Chehłee Van (Chandalar Lake) Koyukon moved westward and settled around Neek'elehno' (South Fork) perhaps at Neeltugh Tene and then to the vicinity of Aalaasuk (Alatna River) after the establishment of the Episcopal Church in Allakaket, Alaska in 1906. One of the last Di'hạiị Gwich'in families in the upper

Koyukuk was met near Jim Creek [(Noon Kuhno' "big porcupine river"[19] (between 1870 and 1898)] by the family of Ida Beatus* who was a child at the time.[20] The Joe Williams (b. 1899[21]) family was the last family to move to Allakaket from the Neek'elehno' (South Fork) area during the first half of the twentieth century (Fig. 33).

Another person on the debtors list is Ch'ijiinjaa, also known as Dihchi' Zhyaa[22] (*zhyaa* means that he was disliked.) His Christian name was John and he was also Too Loghe Hʉt'aane Koyukon. Ch'ijiinjaa was orphaned (from his father) as a young man (twelve[23] or a teenager[24]) and was taken along with his mother and three other women with their children[25] by Dits'ii K'iitł'uu Khaihkwaii after the latter had a run in with some people near the modern day community of Allakaket. McFadyen Clark reported, "c. 1848–1875?: Raids by Kutchin & Tanana people destory Talowa [Too Loghe], Sithleymenket and Dobendaktonten.†"[26] We may discount Too Loghe as it was within Dits'ii K'iitł'uu's own estate and Sełyee Menkk'et[27]

Fig. 33. Joe Williams. Courtesy of Johnson and Bertha Moses.

---

* The mother of Joe Beatus.

† I will use the contemporary spelling for Dobendaktonten, Dobenhdaatltonh Denh throughout.

(Sithleymenket) in the Kk'oonootne (Kanuti) headwaters area. That leaves Dobenhdaatltonh Denh[28] (Elevated Lake[29]) which is near the present day community of Allakaket. Dobenhdaatltonh Denh is the most likely site of this raid. McFadyen Clark has gleaned information about who the actual Koyukon participants might be, but her informants were not certain of their information.[30] It might have been because Ch'ijiinjaa was an older child, but Dits'ii K'iitł'uu had every intention of killing him. His mother, Neeshih, sensing the impending event instructed her son on where to find refuge. Ch'ijiinjaa traveled alone from the Eł tseeyh no' (John River) to the East Fork Chandalar River. There he joined Làrryil,[31] who was also a former Too Loghe Hʉt'aane Koyukon (K'iitł'it Gwich'in) who became a Neets'ąįį Gwich'in, and a relative of his, northwest of Old John Lake (Van K'ehdee,[32] Van K'eedii*) on the East Fork Chandalar River. Ch'ijiinjaa aka Dihch'i'zhyaa became a life long Neets'ąįį Gwich'in. He was a Hudson's Bay Company debtor in 1855 but not in 1851. That means that sometime in the interim he reached the age where he was able to trap and trade for himself, but there are no debtor sheets for the interveneing years. He was holding a feast in 1864.[33] Assuming he was at least twenty years old in 1855, he would have been born about 1835† and was about seventy-one years old when he died in 1906. He appears on the 1900 Census as John Chechejar born circa 1843.‡ If he was twelve years old at the time of the raid on Dobenhdaatltonh Denh, that would have been 1847 or 1848. This story suggests that the Too Logh Hʉt'aane Koyukon takeover of the Di'hąįį estate was sometimes peaceful, through intermarrriage, but also aggressive, and that as early as 1847–48

---

* This means one lake on top of another. Because the lake is very very deep along the shore, but shallow near the northwestern end. I will use this spelling throughout.

† Burch and Mishler thought he was born about 1851. 1995: 157. My father said that Dihch'i'zhyaa was an old man when he died and according to his mother, Soozun Peter, waited for him to be born before he died. My father was born in April of 1906.

‡ Since no one knew their birth dates, the census takers guessed about peoples' ages.

some Koyukon were already living on the Di'hąįį and Neets'ąįį estates.

The name that stands out most on the 1855 Debtors Lists is Tetseekeetlit under Death Outfits. This, I believe, was Dits'ii K'iitł'uu himself. Dits'ii K'iitł'uu means "His/her grandfather came from K'iitł'it (the Koyukuk River headwaters)." His grandfather did come from the Koyukuk River headwaters. As discussed earlier, Dits'ii K'iitł'uu was a Di'hąįį Gwich'in man. His son John Tr'ootsyaa, whose mother was Lucy Shiijuutr'oonyaa,[34] had a caribou fence on the northwestern shores of Van K'eedii (Old John Lake) called Tr'ootsyaa Vatthal.[35] Hadleigh-West thought that it was built sometime between 1869 and 1882.[36] In January of 1866 McDonald mentions Tr'ootsyaa in his journal and that he was looking for a second wife, which meant that, by that time, he probably already had a caribou coral. His younger brother with the same mother, Robert[37] (b. 1851[38])[*] Shoh Vat T'oo [also known as Old Robert, Gamen, and Sakhot'oo (this is a contraction of Shoh Vat T'oo)][39] (Fig. 34) also had a caribou fence on the Koness River (Ch'at'oonjik[†] "nest river") built before 1876. Shoh Vat T'oo was married at Old Rampart on the Porcupine River (Ch'oonjik "porcupine quill river") in 1869.[40] Robert Shoh Vat T'oo was married to Annie Dazhyaa (b. 1849[41]) (Fig. 35) who came from the vicinity of Tanacross, Alaska.[‡] Annie, her older sister Elizabeth Ch'ichyaa Zhuu (White Fox Kit) Solomon, and older brother Joseph Tsal, the father of the late Peter (Weasel Eye) Joseph (b. 1883) of Fort Yukon, and Peter khiahkwaii, whom McDonald called Peter Roe, were all from the middle Tanana River. Robert

---

* Robert may have been older than this.

† The Gwich'in k'oo, kon, and njik all describe the flow of streams. The k'oo is a sluggish body of water like a slough, the kon is the largest body of moving water hence Youk-kon, and njik is a smaller body of water which moves faster (or much faster) than the kon.

‡ Hester Evan, personal communication, 1999. Elizabeth Ch'ichyaa Zhuu Solomon had six children with her first husband, who were left on the Tanana River, when she married Solomon Ndeech'i', a Neets'ąįį Gwich'in man. Elizabeth is Hester Evan's paternal grandmother.

Fig. 34. Robert Shoh Vat T'oo, 1933. Photo taken by Robert A. McKennan. Courtesy of Dartmouth.

Fig. 35. Annie Dazhyaa Roberts from Tanacross area along the Tanana River. Photograph taken in Fort Yukon, Alaska, circa 1920. Courtesy of the Raboff Collection.

and Annie settled at K'ahtsik near the mouth of Teedriinjik (Chandalar River). Tr'ootsyaa and Robert's younger sister Shaanavee Vahan* married John Shoh Tsal (Little Black Bear), one of the youngest of Dahjalti's sons,[42] and one of Shahnyaati's younger brothers with another mother. They raised their family at Fish Camp on the Black River.

Here we can return to McKennan. McKennan knew about the Tanana and Kobuk River connections, but not the Nunataaq (Noatak River) connections.[43] It was difficult for McKennan to piece together the story mainly because he got the movement and migration of people confused with the whole issue of the phratry system and the introduction of language change among the Neets'ąįį Gwich'in. I agree that the migration of people from the Nendaaghe, Too Loghe, and Di'hąįį estates and the people from the middle Tanana River had some influence upon the language. However, the linking of the phratry system with this migration of people and identifying one particular group with a phratry is an erroneous conclusion. McKennan did not have the time to question informants and follow up on answers, nor did he have the assistence of a good interpreter until he arrived in Fort Yukon. I believe Hadleigh-West heard these same stories, followed McKennans lead, and associated them with the phratry system as well. The phratry system among the Neets'ąįį Gwich'in consisted of three groups: Naats'ąįį or Nants'ąįį † (the original inhabitants), Ch'itsyàa (ones helper, someone's helper), and the Tèenjaarahtsyàa (those we bring into the fold). The phratry system predates the nineteenth-century movement and migration of

---

* Shaanavee Vahan did not have a known Christian name, although she probably was baptised. Shaanavee (I can not see clearly, the child had poor eyesight) was the name of her first born child. Vahan (the mother of) identifies her as the mother of Shaanavee. Shaanavee Vahan means "the mother of Shaanavee.' This particular naming system is called teknonymy.

† Two dialect variants. Naats'ąįį is the Nants'ąįį Gwich'in pronunciation which I prefer.

‡ I have extrapolated this from the events which take place in legends from the distant past.

people by 11,000 years or at least until the beginning of the ice recession of the last ice age.‡ Generally speaking the Naats'ąįį and Ch'itsyàa were the dominate phratries. The Tèenjaarahtsyàa were women who married into the society from an outside group that did not have the phratry system (Iñupiat women) or who for various reasons did not know her phratry. The Koyukon, Lower Tanana, and middle Tanana did have the phratry system and they had cognate groups. By example Annie Daazhyaa was of the middle Tanana Ch'echaalyoo (Fish Tail) phratry which translated into the Gwich'in Ch'itsyàa phratry. The phratries were passed on through the woman. If mother was Naats'ąįį, then all of her children—Nm (male) and Nf (female)—would be Naats'ąįį . Ideally Nm would marry a Cf (Ch'itsyàa female) or Tf (Tèenjaarahtsyàa female) and Nf would marry Cm or Tm. They avoided marrying within the same phratry whenever possible. I don't think that there were large numbers of Tèenjaarahtsyàa at any given time. However, I shall return to the Debtors list.

Finally Vats'ach'arathan became a packer between the upper Ch'oonjik (Porcupine) and Peel rivers after 1860, a boatman for the Hudson's Bay Company[44] along the Mackenzie River (Han Gwachoo), and then settled at Fort McPherson, Northwest Territories, Canada.[45] Vats'ach'arathan was known as Vit'ishtr'ijahthan and is the grandfather of the Thompson family of Fort McPherson, Northwest Territories, Canada.[46] He was the oldest brother of John Vindeegwizhii of Fort Yukon (Fig. 36). Vats'acha'ratthan and John Vindeegwizhii were children of Kò'nii'ak (He carries the fire coals).[47] After the Anaktuvuk Pass defeat they joined Dits'ii K'iitł'uu at the mouth of the Eł tseeyh no' (John River) along with other Koyukon women and children. Years later, in the late 1920s, John Vindeegwizhii confronted Panniaq, Elijah Kakinya, and Billy Morry in Fort Yukon and told them that he was a small boy when the raid took place at K'iitł'it/ Anaktuvuk Pass. As stated earlier, since Simon Panniaq Paneak was an Iñupiat historian, this many have cemented his notion that the Gwich'in were the ones

Fig. 36. John Vindeeegwizhii, c. 1933. Photograph taken by Robert A. McKennan. Courtesy of Dartmouth.

known as the Uyaġaaġmiut. John Vindeegwizhii became a Di'hąįį Gwich'in because he was raised on the Di'hąįį estate by Dits'ii K'iitł'uu. Kǫ̀'nii'ak was a K'iitł'it Gwich'in (Koyukon) man who must have died during the late 1840s because Dits'ii K'iitł'uu raised and adopted Vindeegwizhii and Vats'ach'aratthan.[48] At one point he brought back a bride for Vats'ach'aratthan, but the latter had already gone on to Peel River and asked that the bride be given to John Deeghoozhraii (large dark eyes), the son of Sarah Shaaghan Dik. John Deeghoozhraii was an infant or toddler during the flight from K'iitł'it/Anaktuvuk Pass.[49] Deeghoozhraii married the young woman who became known only as Ch'ich'i'tsoo Vahan (the mother of brown/blond hair), since Ch'ich'i'tsoo was their little girl's name.

Deeghoozhraii became known as Ch'ich'i'tsooti',[50] the father of Ch'ich'i'tsoo. The mother and child died of an illness during the early 1860s. Ch'ich'i'tsoo Vahan was taken during a raid down the Koyukuk River by Dits'ii K'iitł'uu, possibly at Dobenhdaatltonh Denh (1847). She probably grew into adulthood with the Di'hąįį Gwich'in and had been promised to Vats'ach'arathan.

These are all very important findings that tell us more about the relationship between the Nendaaghe and Too Loghe Hut'aane Koyukon and the Di'hąįį , Draanjik, and Neets'ąįį Gwich'in than we would have known otherwise. Through examination of the rosters and the genealogical information provided by the late Steven Tsee Gho' Tsyaa Tsal Peter, Sr., we have been able to piece together the movement of people ravaged by diseases, famine, internal warfare, and battling for the maintenance of their estates. These reports are of the Di'hąįį estate northern boundary activities.We can now turn our attention to the Lower Ramparts and Olsons Lake.

What Happened in the Lower Ramparts, 1847–51

Alexander Hunter Murray reported in the spring of 1848 that, "None of the lower band were here since April, they are passing the spring with the "Tannin-Kootchin' on the other side of the [Tsee Choo] mountains to the west of this, and I have heard, have disposed of many of their furs to that band [Menhtee Xut'ana] for beads...I fully expected to have prevented the Indians here from meeting them, and it was my policy and is still, however repugnant to my feelings to encourage [rather?] than otherwise the enmity between the Kootcha-Kootchin and lower bands."[51] The first lower band, in this instance, was the lower band of the Gwichyaa Gwich'in— Shahnyaati's band. Shahnyaati's regional band was known as the

---

* "Deenduu is an old word; the meaning is not known. However, Duu nąįį was another old phrase for the Teets'ii Gwich'in the Koyukon." Katherine Peter, personal communication, 1999. *Deenduu* is probably a contracted word, *dee nduhts'ąįį*, meaning "people above those on the other side of the river." Or it could be a contracted word with *Duu*, indicating Koyukon inhabitants.

Deenduu Gwich'in.* The second lower bands are the Taghe Chox
Xut'ana Lower Tanana, Di'hąįį Gwich'in, Menhtee Xut'ana Lower
Tanana on the Minto Flats, and all the other Koyukon nations on the
Koyukuk and Yukon rivers below Fort Yukon. Murray did indeed
encourage enmity and he found the perfect Gwich'in ally in the "little
chief," Shahnyaati', who was already well known for his aggressive
disposition[52] throughout the Yukon Flats.

Long before the actual arrival of the Hudson's Bay Company at
Fort Yukon, the Western Gwich'in* went through a period of internal
fueding. The introduction of new trade items from the north, west,
south, and east triggered a bid for which families would control the
trade routes. The fighting began as early as 1805–06 with the
establishment of Fort Good Hope on the Mackenzie River (Han
Gwachoo) and included both the Eastern and Western Gwich'in
nations. The internal feuding took place along phratry lines. In other
words, members of the different phratries began to feud. These feuds
continued until at least the 1830s. I believe that Murray alluded to
this feuding when he stated, "twenty years ago, they say they were
a large nation, but being always at war more than half of their people
have been killed."[53] The upshot was that the large polygamous
household of Dahjalti'[54] prevailed among the Western Gwich'in and
his sons took over the trade routes from the headwaters of the
Ch'oonjik (Porcupine River) to the Lower Ramparts on the Yukon
River.† One of Dahjalti's older sons was Shahnyaati', the young chief
whom Murray praised as such a good fort hunter.[55] Shahnyaati' (Fig.
37) became the most famous of Gwich'in trading chiefs, from before
1847 to the day of his death in 1894.[56] He traded mostly in the Yukon
Flats, but went to the Lower Tanana (1848) and to the Arctic Ocean[57]
(1849) trading for furs that he in turn sold to the Hudson's Bay
Company at Fort Yukon, much to the disapproval of Murray[58] and

---

* Western Gwich'in are those within the State of Alaska; Eastern Gwich'in are those
in northwestern Canada.
† There is every reason to believe that the Koyukon and Lower Tanana went through
a similar process.

Fig. 37. Etching of Shahnyaati' near the old Fort at Fort Yukon, Alaska, c. 1883. Courtesy of Anchorage Historical Museum.

Hardisty[59] who were quite agitated by what they regarded as his interfering with trade at Fort Yukon. Shahnyaati' was so well known that Raymond, mentioned earlier, named a village after him, Senati Village.[60] For Murray and Hardisty, Shahnyaati' was useful as a hunter, informant, and an instrument of their sowing aggression among the nations. On the other hand, Shahnyaati' was also a major annoyance and hindrance in the conduct of their business at the fort.[61]

In 1843, the Too Loghe Hut'aane Koyukon and the Di'hąįį Gwich'in (Too Tleekk'e Hut'aane), we learned, were in the habit of trading at the mouth of the Koyukuk River and often returned by way of the Yukon River. They were behaving as middlemen for the people above the confluence of the Tanana and Yukon rivers, mainly the people further up the Yukon and Porcupine rivers—the Taghe Chox Xut'ana Lower Tanana, Neets'ąįį, Deenduu, Gwichyaa, Draanjik, Vantee and Dagǫǫ Gwich'in, and the Han. One of Hadleigh-West's informants maintained that the Di'hąįį Gwich'in "did secure some Russian goods."[62] The Yookkene and Noghee Hut'aane

Koyukon, along the Yukon River above Nulato, were conducting their own trade at Nulato and also acting as middlemen for those who lived further up the river. The Menhtee Xut'ana Lower Tanana also conducted trade with the Russians.[63] They traded Russian merchandise in exchange for furs which they in turn traded to the Russians in Nulato. The various nations gathered at Noochu Loghoyet (Łiidlạii in Gwich'in[64]) at the confluence of the Tanana and Yukon rivers sometime after break-up in early June. However, all of this changed after the establishment of the Hudson's Bay Company at Fort Yukon in 1847.

The establishment of the Hudson's Bay Company in Fort Yukon changed the patterns of trade among the various Interior nations. (Katherine Arndt covered this thoroughly in her Master's Thesis: *Dynamics of the Fur Trade on the Middle Yukon River, Alaska, 1839 to 1868, 1996*). The Too Loghe Hut'aane Koyukon and Di'hạii Gwich'in (Dits'ii K'iitł'uu and Gook'ạahtii's communities and/or regional bands), who traded at the mouth of the Koyukuk River and returned up the Yukon to trade at the Lower Ramparts, began to see their business dwindle. Furthermore, they incurred the enmity of the Menhtee Xut'ana Lower Tanana (Minto Flats) who also traded in Nulato and whom they were in direct competition with. It seems that before 1847, the ties between the Too Loghe Hut'aane Koyukon and Di'hạii Gwich'in with the Kodeel Kkaakk'e Hut'aane Koyukon near the mouth of the Koyukuk River were stronger than afterwards. It appears that after the Nendaaghe and Too Loghe Hut'aane Koyukon defeats in the Brooks Range, they began to encroach upon the Di'hạii estate. The Nendaaghe and Too Loghe Hut'aane Koyukon were on the Di'hạii estate to the north of Chehłee Van (Chandalar Lake) middle to late 1840s and were already established up the Kk'oonootne (Kanuti River). The Koyukon, about the Aalaasuk (Alatna River) and Kk'oonootne (Kanuti) rivers, may have made an attempt to join their relatives at Chandalar Lake or to oust Dits'ii K'iitł'uu who was between them and the other band of Too Loghe Hut'aane Koyukon at Chandalar Lake. This certainly would have incurred Dits'ii

K'iitɬ'uu's wrath. Concurrently the Too Loghe Hʉt'aane Koyukon at Chehɬee Van (Chandalar Lake) continued to have egress past Dits'ii K'iitɬ'uu to the Lower Koyukuk for in 1847 they descended the Koyukuk River and presumably returned up the Yukon. In the company of Shahnyaati', two of them went to Fort Yukon with rumors about the Russians, much to the mortification of Murray.[65] I think it was because of Shahnyaati's presence that the Too Loghe Hʉt'aane Koyukon passed through Gook'ąąhtii's range along the Lower Ramparts. At the time Shahnyaati' was beginning to take control of who had access to the fort from down the river.

The change in trade routes had all the nations embroiled in conflict. Although the Menhtee and Taghe Chox Xut'ana Lower Tanana nations shared the north and south slopes of the Tsee Choo Dhah (Big Beaver Mountains), according to Murray they were at war with each other during the winter of 1848.[66] Peter John (of Minto, Alaska) made two statements on two separate occasions that might shed light on this. In the first statement he stated that the Taghe Chox Xut'ana Lower Tanana were at one time living above Big Minto Lake.[67] In the second statement, which is also pertinent, the war at Tohot'onhde, the Morelock Creek war site,[68] happened before the two wars on the Minto Flats at Dextso degh'o on the Lower Chantanika River and at Menok'oget (the site of New Minto).[69] It is very likely that the Di'hąįį Gwich'in along the Yukon River were involved with the Tohot'onhde war since as it was within their estate and range. They would have joined forces with the Taghe Chox Xut'ana Lower Tanana, but not with the Menhtee Xut'ana Lower Tanana. Their reasons would have been (1) the Menhtee Xut'ana Lower Tanana were at a greater distance from them, (2) they were probably more closely related to members of the Taghe Chox Xut'ana Lower Tanana, (3) they needed the free range along the Yukon River, (4) the Menhtee Xut'ana Lower Tanana had elicited the aide of the Yookkene and Noghee Hʉ'taane Koyukon from further down the Yukon River because they needed passage down the Yukon River to Nulato and they were probably trading partners, and (5) The Taghe

Chox Xut'ana Lower Tanana were probably the Di'hạị̣ Gwich'in partners in trade. If this were the case in 1847, Dits'ii K'iitł'uu khaihkwaii made a raid upon the Too Loghe Hut'aane Koyukon at Dobenhdaatltonh Denh along the Koyukuk River and his son, Gook'ạ̇ạhtii Khaihkwaii, allied himself with the Taghe Chox Xut'ana Lower Tanana, and were having a major battle at Tohot'onhde (Morelock Creek) with the Menhtee Xut'ana Lower Tanana and their Koyukon allies. In an interesting note, de Laguna stated: "I was told by Mrs. Coulombe, of Kalland, that there is said to have been a battle between the local Indians [Noghee Hut'aane Koyukon] and invaders from the Kobuck River."[70] If anyone was being identified as coming from the Kobuk it would have been the Nendaaghe and Too Loghe Hut'aane Koyukon who were by that time essentially one nation living in two localities—the area of the Aalaasuk (Alatna River) and Chehłee Van (Chandalar Lake). Plus the Koyukon, who had recently joined the Di'hạị̣ Gwich'in, were from the Kobuk, Nunataaq (Noatak), and Kuukpik (Colville) rivers. Why the Kobuk River was emphasized must have been because of the recent Nendaaghe Hut'aane Koyukon presence in the upper Kobuk and that some 'Saakił Hut'aane Koyukon did move to the east with them. The Di'hạị̣ Gwich'in were fighting on two fronts, along the Koyukuk and Yukon rivers in 1847. The war at Tohot'onhde was a major event, a turning point for all the nations involved.

Murray reported in 1848 that, "The lower band [Deenduu Gwich'in] of this nation was at war as I have already mentioned with the 'Teytse-Kootchin' and five of the latter were killed, but not in open battle, a regular 'stand up fight' seldom occurs, the usual mode is by surprise at night [they decide to fight the Teytse-Kootchin]...Upwards of thirty warriors started off in canoes, on their way down they had put ashore to sleep, when five of the unsuspecting "Teytse-Kootchin' arrived [They killed the five warriors]...The warriors (murderers) [Shahnyaati'] proceeded on their journey intending to have still further revenge, but they returned here with out killing more, there were too many of the other Indians together for them to attack successfully."[71] The same ambush is recounted by François Xavier Mercier, but in his version he claims that they were Neets'ąįį Gwich'in (Murray's Teytse-Kootchin) and that they "were fishing for salmon in the large eddy which is found at the foot of the rapids [Morelock Creek], called the first rampart of the Youkon, about 45 miles up stream from the Noukelakayet Station [Old Tanana Mission at the mouth of Tozitna River], and that at the same time Sénaté [Shahnyaati'] was camped with his men at the head of the same ramparts [near Bear Creek]."[72] John Taylor White, aboard the *Revenue Steamer Nunivak* in 1898–1900, says, "It seems that war broke out between these people and the warlike Tananas in which the Koyukons probably joined."[73] Apparently, Shahnyaati' was on the periphery of the battle at Tohot'onhde, but he killed five people; who were these people? We will return to this story later.

Consequently Shahnyaati' khaihkwaii, recognizing the crux of the situation, wasted no time in forming an alliance with the Menhtee Xut'ana Lower Tanana. Shahnyaati' spent the spring of 1848 with the Menhtee Xut'ana on the Minto Flats. However, Shahnyaati' also went hunting in the mountains to the southwest of Fort Yukon for caribou,[74] which was well within his own estate, but a shared range with the Menhtee and Taghe Chox Xut'ana Lower Tanana. Then, in the following spring, he went to the Arctic Ocean with the Neets'ąįį Gwich'in with good reason—he was related to the Neets'ąįį Gwich'in people. Shahnyaati' was setting the stage to dominate the trade in the Lower Ramparts. By September of 1849, Murray was fully expecting the *gens de bute* (Menhtee Xut'ana) to be traveling with Shahnyaati', but Shahnyaati' reported that he had not seen the Menhtee Xut'ana Lower Tanana that fall. To what extent Murray had a role in this alliance we will never know. Certainly the Menhtee Xut'ana and those further up on the Tanana were a large group; Murray numbered them at upwards of 100 men.[75] To entice these people away from trade with the Russians and to Fort Yukon certainly would have been profitable to the Hudson's Bay Company.

In March of 1849 the Taghe Chox Xut'ana were among Shahnyaati's Deenduu Gwich'in, trying to enlist mercenaries "to go to war with them against the men of the shade [Koyukon]."[76] The interpreter, Antoine Hoole, thought that only one or two would go. The term Teets'ii Gwich'in had two meanings: (1) for the Koyukon in general and (2) for anyone downriver from where the speaker is. In this instance, we should gather that "men of the shade," although it sounds specific, should be taken to mean anyone downriver. That would include the Noghee, Too Loghe, and Yookkene Hʉt'aane Koyukon and Menhtee Xut'ana or Di'hąįį Gwich'in. For a nation consisting of twenty men, the Taghe Chox Xut'ana Lower Tanana were very busy with warfare during the winter of 1847–48, and preparing for warfare in March of 1849.

One year later in March of 1850, Murray reports of the Taghe Chox Xut'ana, "There has been a great fight between them with the middle Indians and another band (of) Indians there and the run in which 20 (15 men and 5 women) of the latter were killed."[77] This may be connected to Leonard John's version, "those people that lived here [near Stevens Village] got together and went over to Koyukuk River and killed some people there. When they came back they were afraid the people of the Koyukuk would follow them over and kill them off, so they prepared themselves with a wooden fence all around their camp, so that their enemies wouldn't come near them."[78] This is the battle which can be interfaced with the annihilation of people at Sełyee Menkk'et (Sethleymenkat) along the upper Kk'oonootne (Kanuti River). McFadyen Clark's informants were not sure which community Hʉdughyenee's[79] (Hotoyeni) parents were killed at: Sełyee Menkk'et or Dobenhdaatltonh Denh. It was most likely Sełyee Menkk'et. Hʉdughyenee was married and had moved away from the community to live with her husband's people near the mouth of the Aalaasuk (Alatna River). The people of Sełyee Menkk'et were Too Loghe Hʉt'aane Koyukon. Later Murray follows up, "this band [Taghe Chox Xut'ana] intended going to meet the Russians as usual, but they were disappointed last year and are now afraid of the Indians further down, with whom those here have been at war."[80] This last statement suggests that Shahnyaati' and/or some of his men, acting as mercenaries, joined in the attack on Sełyee Menkk'et as Antoine Hoole thought they would. Leonard John continued, "That fall a big army of Koyukuk people came over, but they couldn't come near the camp, so they let them go. When the people from the Koyukuk had gone back, the people that were here moved away and there was nobody here [at the mouth of Dall River] for years."[81] In McKennan's notes, Henry John[82] of Venetie states that, "Dihaii: Lived on ridge between Chandalar and Koyukuk. Once swooped down on village (25 miles below Stevens Village) and cleaned it out…" In this particular instance Henry John is referring to the Too Loghe Hʉt'aane Koyukon at Chandalar Lake, not to Dits'ii K'iitł'uu. The Taghe Chox Xut'ana did not move right away.

Meanwhile, during the winter of 1849–50, there was an areawide famine and illness which affected every nation that traded at Fort Yukon. Murray's entries after January 1850[83] tell of famine among the Draanjik along the Black River. In March 1850 he states the Neets'ạii and Vantee (or Dagǫǫ) Gwich'in were reduced to eleven men and nine boys. In June 1850 Murray writes: "…(Suffering amongst the Indians to the west) one band I believe of the Tchukootchi have all except two men died of starvation…" Murray was guessing; it could not have been the Taghe Chox Xut'ana, because late in June eight of them show up to trade.[84] If anyone was reduced to two men in 1850, it would have been the Too Loghe Hʉt'aane Koyukon along the upper Kk'oonootne (Kanuti) and near the mouth of the Aalaasuk (Alatna River). That was one band of the the Too Loghe Hʉt'aane Koyukon, the others being at Chehłee Van (Chandalar Lake).

In July of 1850 some "strange Indians" arrive from below. Murray was expecting them to return in the fall as they were in the habit of trading with the Russians. Murray saved some guns for them, "The few guns now in store are kept purposely as an encouragement to those Lower Indians when they come in fall, as an inducement to make them bring their furs here rather than take them to the Russians."[85] The Too Loghe Hut'aane Koyukon made their first visit to the fort. They arrived in the company of Shahnyaati'. Their presence on the Yukon Flats caused some consternation among the fort regulars.[86] Shahnyaati's younger brother already had two guns but wanted another one; he was refused. No doubt this must have angered Shahnyaati', for he became increasingly difficult to settle with. Meanwhile the Too Loghe Hut'aane Koyukon started frequenting the fort; five returned in October, 1850 and three came in February 1851 to trade.[87] This was a significant move. This supported the Iñupiat notion that Fort Yukon people were related to the people on the upper Kobuk in the early twentieth century. However, they were people who moved into the Yukon Flats area; they did not originate on the Yukon Flats.

On March 1, 1851 news came of another battle. "Four Indians from mountains west of this [traded]...they received a gun and ammunition in payment...These poor fellows live by themselves in the mountains, being all that remains of a large band, while these four (two men and two boys) were off hunting, all their friends were killed by the Mountain Indians from below. This is the first time they visited the fort."[88] This was the battle at Too Loghe (Talowa) on Olsons Lake at the head of the Kanuti, Ray, and Dall rivers. The Menhtee Xut'ana Lower Tanana and Shahnyaati's Deenduu Gwich'in were the perpetrators. After their tangle with the Menhtee Xut'ana in 1847 it's very unlikely that the Taghe Chox Xut'ana were involved in this attack. McFadyen Clark's informants claimed that the invaders were "Kutchin ('Fort Yukon men') or by Indians from the Tanana River."[89] Alexander, one of those survivors, must have been about six years old at the time if he was born circa 1845.[90] His mother and other brothers and sister were taken to the Yukon River. McFadyen Clark's informants stated that Alexander's Iñupiaq name was Doyuk. Hudughyenee's siblings were also taken away from Sełyee Menkk'et.

---

* Another guess by the census takers.

One person who may be related to both Alexander and Hʉdughyenee is Dihch'i' George (b. 1845[91]),* the grandfather of the late Kilbourn George of Stevens Village, Alaska. If we recall Dits'ii K'iitł'uu took Neeshih and her son, John Chijiinjaa, along with the three women and their children from Dobenhdaatltonh Denh. Dihch'i' George was the adopted or biological son of Dits'ii K'iitł'uu with one of the other women (not Neeshih). In 1864, when he was older (maybe fifteen or older), he went to Fort Yukon with Vats'ach'arathan and his brother John Vindeegwizhii, then later settled down near Stevens Village as an adult. No doubt he settled among people he recognized as relatives. Kilbourn George was not sure of the connection, but stated that they (his grandfather and others of the older generation) "came from Allakaket area."[92]

Shahnyaati' had been allying himself with the Menhtee Xut'ana Lower Tanana since at least 1847, but the relationship could have been going on much longer, since the trade route between the Tseenjik (Beaver) and Chatanika rivers must have predated that. Shahnyaati' finally had his opportunity to revenge himself upon the Di'haii Gwich'in whom he had been hoping to avenge since 1847 when his attempt was aborted at Tohot'onhde (Morelock Creek). Shahnyaati's foiled attempt at Tohot'onhde must have been a major sore point. According to Murray, Shahnyaati' left with thirty canoes of warriors but was forced to return because of the numbers of the party at Tohot'onhde. To gather a war-party cost beads and trade items and it was not likely that Shahnyaati' would forget that soon. If we recall, Mercier said that it was the Neets'aii Gwich'in who recounted this story of five of their number being murdered by Shahnyaati'. I have explained this elsewhere,[93] but this bears repetition. People became members of whatever estate they happened to live in or they became known as residents of that estate even if they did not regard themselves as such. Here are three examples: (1) John Ch'ijiinjaa was a Too Loghe Hʉt'aane Koyukon from the Aalaasuk (Alatna River) area by birth. He was abducted during a raid to the Di'haii estate, but passed on to the Neets'aii estate. He spent the rest of his life on the Neets'ąįį estate and became known as a Neets'ąįį Gwich'in person. (2) Aldzak, the father of Sarah Shaaghan Dik and her half sister Naach'ats'an (different mothers), who both became wives of Dits'ii K'iitł'uu, was Nendaaghe Hut'aane Koyukon (Fig. 39). He traveled through the Too Loghe estate and finally settled as a recluse on a mountain near Chehłee Van (Chandalar Lake) on the Di'hąįį estate. My father, Steven Peter, Sr., thought that it might have been on Horace Mountain to the west of Chandalar Lake. Aldzak became known as a Di'hąįį Gwich'in person. (3) Làrryil, the father of Christian Choo, was either a Nendaaghe or Too Loghe Hut'aane Koyukon who moved onto the Neets'ąįį estate (probably through marriage) and became known as a Neets'ąįį Gwich'in. The upshot is that, in 1847, Shahnyaati' killed five Di'hąįį Gwich'in who might have been Too Loghe Hut'aane Koyukon, whose families later ended up on the Neets'ąįį estate.

Meanwhile at the mouth of the Koyukuk River something else was happening which changed the makeup of the Koyukuk River communities. The internal warfare between the Kodeel Kkaakk'e Hut'aane Koyukon at the mouth of Kateel River and those Koyukon

Fig. 38. Unknown Koyukon family near the Neek'elehno' (South Fork Koyukuk River), 1899. Probably Too Loghe Hut'aane Koyukon. Courtesy of F.C. Schrader, USGS.

Fig. 39. Aldzak Family Tree.

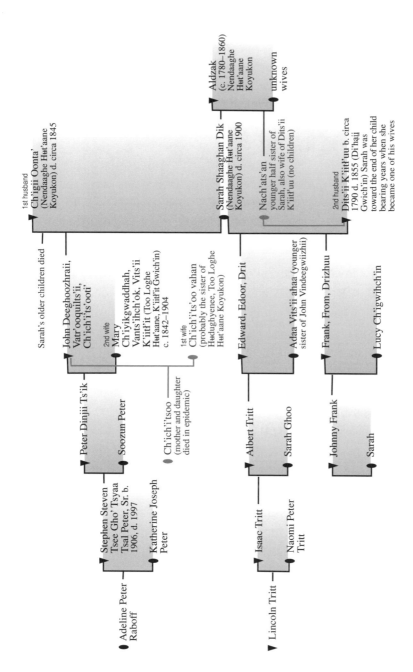

Fig. 40. Two boys from Bettles, Alaska. L to R an Indian boy and an Iñupiaq boy. Courtesy of the Charles E. Bunnell Collection, University of Alaska Fairbanks.

nations lower on the Yukon River in 1851,[94] impacted life on the Koyukuk River. Jette states, "When they [the warriors] returned [to Kodeel Kkaak'et] after the massacre, they fled as fast as they could with their families up to Nararadotiłten [Naahaaghedoteeł Denh[95]]*, and thence overland to the Koyukuk River."[96] McFadyen Clark reported that after the raid in Nulato, "several of the Kateel families moved northward to the Huslia-Dalbi-Hogatza band region. The reason for this movement were two fold: (1) fear of reprisals from the Nulato people and (2) increase in trade between Koyukuk Indians and Kobuk Eskimos with whalers at Kotzebue Sound."[97] So after 1851 some Kodeel Kkaakk'e Hut'aane Koyukon families moved up the Koyukuk River and settled in below Kk'oonootne (Kanuti River). They were trading with the Hulghaatne Hut'aane Iñupiat on the Kobuk River and with the Siivḷium Kaŋianiġmiut at the Siilivik (Selawik River) headwaters. The increase in whaling ships along the coast after 1848[98] greatly increased the amount of goods coming into the upper Koyukuk River valley. The area above the Kk'oonootne (Kanuti River) near Aalaasuk (Alatna River) was sparsely populated at the time.

---

* Louden between Galena and Kokrines along the Yukon River.

Part 4, Chapter Notes

1. Simon Paneak, tape 842, transcript, University of New Mexico, Center for Southwest Research, September 1971: 1–3.

2. Helge Ingstad, *Nunamiut*, (New York: W. W. Norton & Company, 1954): 32.

3. Simon Paneak, tape 844, transcript, University of New Mexico, Center for Southwest Research, September 1971: 11.

4. Nicholas J. Gubser, *"Comparative Study of the Intellectual Culture of the Nunamiut Eskimos at Anaktuvuk Pass, Alaska,"* (Fairbanks: University of Alaska, 1961): 88.

5. Paneak, tape 844, transcript, 1971: 11.

6. Gubser (1961): 88.

7. STP, 1987–97.

8. Ibid.

9. 1900 Census, University of Alaska Archives.

10. Hudson Bay Company Archives, B.240/a/3: fo. 17d.

11. Robert McKennan, *The Chandalar Kutchin*, Arctic Institute of North America Technical Paper No. 17 (New York, 1965): 24.

12. McDonald, journal entry, 12 March 1867 (1910) .

13. STP, Ch'iji'oonta' vizheh k'aa, 1987–97.

14. STP, 1987–97.

15. STP, the father of the late Sophie Paul of Fort Yukon, Alaska, 1987–97.

16. 1920 Census.

17. Alexander Hunter Murray, *Journal of the Yukon 1847–48*, (Ottawa: Government Printing Bureau, 1910): 62.

18. McDonald, journal entry, 20 February 1867.

19. *Upper Koyukuk River Place Names* (Fairbanks: Alaska Native Language Center Library, University of Alaska, n.d.)

20. Ernest S. Burch, Jr., and Craig W. Mishler, "The Di'haii Gwich'in: Mystery People of Northern Alaska," *Arctic Anthropology* 32, no. 1 (1995): 159.

21. 1900 Census, Territory of Alaska.

22. STP, Dits'ii K'iitł'uu vizheh k'aa, 1987–97.

23. Isaac Tritt, personal communication, 1995; Burch and Mishler, 1995: 156.

24. STP, 1987–97. My father said that Ch'ijiinjaa was "a teenager."

25. STP, 1987–97; Burch and Mishler (1995): 18.

26. McFadyen Clark, *Who Lived in This House? A Study of Koyukuk river Semisubterranean Houses*, Mercury Series, Archaelogical Survey of Canada, Paper 153. (Quebec: Canadian Museum of Civilization, 1996): 18.

27. James M. Kari, personal communication, 1999.

28. McFadyen Clark (1996): 65. Also Dobenhdaatltonh Den.

29. Eliza Jones, personal communication, 1999.

30. McFadyen Clark (1996): 65.

31. STP, 1987–97.

32. Richard A. Caulfield and Walter Peter, Subsistence Division, Alaska Department of Fish and Game, U. S. Geological Survey 250,000 series Maps, 1982: item 26.

33. McDonald, journal entry, 31 April 1910.

34. McKennan (1965: 24). He erroneously thought that she was a Yukon Flats Kutchin.

35. STP, 1987–97.

36. Hadleigh-West, "The Netsi Kutchin: An Essay in Human Ecology," (Ph. D. diss. in Anthropology, Louisiana State University and Agricultural and Mechanical College, Baton Rouge, Louisiana, 1963): 313

37. Cyndie Warbelow, David Roseneau and Peter Stern, "The Kutchin Caribou Fences of Northeastern Alaska And The Northern Yukon," Biological Report Series Volume Thirty Two, in *Studies of Large Mammals Along the Proposed Mackenzie Valley Gas Pipeline Route From Alaska to British Columbia*, ed. R. D. Jakimchuk (October 1975): 88.

38. 1900 Census, Territory of Alaska under Fish Camp, Gens-de-large, Kutchin.

39. STP, Dits'ii K'iitł'uu vizheh k'aa, 1987–97.

40. Burch and Mishler (1995): 158.

41. 1900 census, Territory of Alaska.

42. STP, 1987–97.

43. McKennan (1965): 61.

44. STP, 1987–97; John T. Ritter, personal communication, 1999.

45. John T. Ritter, personal communication, 1999.

46. Ibid.

47. Johnny and Sarah Frank, *Neerihiinjik: We Traveled From Place to Place*, ed. Craig Mishler (Fairbanks: Alaska Native Language Center, University of Alaska Fairbanks, 1995): 677; STP, Kò'nii'ak vizheh k'aa, 1987–97.

48. STP, 1987–97.

49. STP, McKennan field notes, University of Alaska Archives, 1987–97.

50. STP, Ch'ich'i'tsooti' vizheh k'aa, 1987–97.

51. Murray (1910): 92.

52. William Schneider, *Beaver, Alaska: The Story of a Multi-Ethnic Community*, paper submitted to the faculty of Bryn Mawr College, 1976: 315–326; François Xavior Mercier, *"Recollections of the Youkon; Memoires from the Years 1868–1885,"* ed. Linda Finn Yarborough (Anchorage: The Alaska Historical Society, 1986): 54, 56.

53. Murray (1910): 88.

54. Ibid.: 86. I believe that Murray made a passing reference to Dahjalti'. "The principal men of the nation have two and three wives each, one old leader here has five…"

55. Ibid.: 98.

56. McDonald, journal entry, 9 April 1894 (1910).

57. HBCA, B.240/a/3, Id, journal entry for 4 July 1849.

58. Murray, journal entry, 6 June 1849: B.240/a/3; 4 July 1849, HBCA 1849; Id, 10 October 1849, 12 July 1850: HBCA, B.240/a/3.

59. William L. Hardisty, letter dated 10 November 1857, HBCA, d. 532: 237–37

60. Captain Charles W. Raymond, *Report of a Reconnaissance of the Yukon River, Alaska Territory, July to September, 1869* (Washington: Government Press Office, 1871): 22.

61. Katherine Louise Arndt, "Dynamics of the Fur Trade of the Middle Yukon River, Alaska, 1839–1868," (thesis, Fairbanks, Alaska, 1996): 131–135.

62. Hadleigh-West (1963): 262.

63. Murray (1910): 83.

64. Katherine Peter, personal communication, 1999.

65. Murray (1910): 67.

66. Murray (1910): 72; HBCA, B.240/a/1, 35d.

67. Peter John, interview by Bill Schneider, tape #H88-41B, 29 April 1988.

68. Frederica de Laguna, *The Prehistory of Northern North America as Seen From the Yukon*, The Society For American Archaeology, no. 3, Of Memoirs of the Society (Menasha, Wisconsin, 1947): 39.

69. Peter John, interview with James M. Kari, 1999.

70. de Laguna (1947): 39.

71. Murray (1910): 87.

72. Mercier (1986): 54, 56.

73. John Taylor White, "Synopsis of Dall River Indians," University of Alaska, n.d.: 7.

74. HBCA, 240/1/3, fo. 18.

75. Murray (1910): 83.

76. HBCA, B.240/a/2.

77. HBCA, B.240/a/3.

78. Leonard John, "How Stevens Village Came To Be," *Alaska Sportsman*, (September 1959): 32.

79. McFadyen Clark (1996): 63.

80. HBCA, B.240/a/4.

81. John (1959).

82. STP, Ch'ich'i'tsooti vizheh k'aa, 1987–97.

83. HBCA, B.240/a/3.

84. HBCA, B.240/a/4.

85. HBCA, B.240/a/4.

86. HBCA, entry for July 1850, B.240/a/4.

87. HBCA, B.240/a/4.

88. HBCA, B.240/a/4, 18d.

89. McFadyen Clark (1996): 62–63

90. Ibid.: 66.

91. 1900 census, Territory of Alaska under Stevens Village.

92. Kilbourn George, personal communication, 1991.

93. Raboff (1999): 20.

94. Arndt, 1996: 103–108; de Laguna, 1947: 52; Jette, history ms, untitled notes on Ten'a Superstition, 1914, 1905: 25; William J. Loyens, *The changing Culture of the Nulato Koyukon Indians* (Ph.D. diss., University of Wisconsin, Madison, University of Microfilms, Ann Arbor, Michigan, 1975); McFadyen Clark (1974): 187–191 and (1996): 22; Robert McDonald, in Church Missionary Record, Vol. 2, December 1872: 398–99; Miranda Wright, "The Last Great Indian War, Nulato 1851," (master's thesis, Department of Anthropology, University of Alaska Fairbanks, 1995).

95. Kari, personal communication, 1999.

96. Jette, 1905: 25.

97. Annette McFadyen Clark, ed., "Upper Koyukuk River Koyukon Athapaskan Social Culture: an Overview," proceedings: Northern Athapaskan Conference, 1971, Vol. 1.

98. John R. Bockstoce, *Whales, Ice & Men: The History of Whaling in the Western Arctic* (Seattle: University of Washington Press in association with the New Bedford Whaling Museum, University of Washington Department of Printing, 1986).

The Aftermath

These shifts in power between 1847 and 1851 changed the makeup of all the nations surrounding Fort Yukon. Murray noted that the Gwichyaa Gwich'in said that they were once a large nation, but through warfare had been reduced to half their number some twenty years before the establishment of the fort (circa 1820s).[1] At the time (1847) the Deenduu, Draanjik, and Gwichyaa Gwich'in together numbered ninety men. The periods of famine and illness during this period (1849–51) and the scarlet fever epidemic of 1865 further decreased the population in the whole area.

The Nendaaghe and Too Loghe Hʉt'aane Koyukon were in two regional bands by 1847. The first regional band was at Chehłee Van (Chandalar Lake) and another extended from the mouth of the Aalaasuk (Alatna River) to the upper Kk'oonootne (Kanuti River).[*] The Aalaasuk (Alatna River) regional band began to push up the Kk'oonootne (Kanuti River). The Di'hąįį Gwich'in patriarch, Dits'ii K'iitł'uu, wiped out the community of Dobenhdaatltonh Denh near the mouth of the Aalaasuk (Alatna River) in 1847 and took away Dihch'i' George's mother, Neeshih and John Ch'ijiinjaa as a youth along with other children and two women. This was a Gwich'in/Koyukon conflict. Why Dits'ii K'iitł'uu did not have the same warlike behavior towards the Koyukon group on Chehłee Van (Chandalar Lake) is a mystery. Perhaps this group was more

---

* I do not believe the Kk'oonootne Hʉt'aane Koyukon were a separate regional band at the time.

intermarried with his family.

In March of 1850 the Taghe Chox Xut'ana wiped out the community of Sełyee Menkk'et along the upper Kk'oonootne (Kanuti River). The upper Koyukuk River, at least below the Eł tseeyh no' (John River) was sparsely populated in the early 1840s. This allowed room for the Hułghaatne Hut'aane Iñupiat (upper Kobuk) to start moving into the Aalaasuk (Alatna River) headwaters. The Iñupiat moved down the Aalaasuk (Alatna River) and made connections with their Kuukpiġmiut relatives now on the abandoned Nendaaghe and northern Too Loghe estates. The Kuukpiġmiut developed a feasting relationship with the Too Loghe Hut'aane Koyukon living near the mouth of the Eł tseeyh no' (John River) after 1870.[2]

Meanwhile, after the 1851 raid on Nulato, several Kodeel Kkaakk'e Hut'aane Koyukon (Kateel River nation) families moved up the river into the Huslia-Dalbi-Hogatza* nation. The Huslia-Dalbi-Hogatza nation absorbed Alexander and Hudughyenee. "A second movement occurred about 1860–75 when several Huslia-Dalbi-Hogatza families moved north and joined the Kanuti-Todadonten band near the mouth of the Kanuti River [perhaps at Hor-tar-chaket or Kornuchaket]. Along with this later movement, some members from the upper Kanuti component of the South Fork band moved to the same region."[3] McFadyen Clark was more specific, "Earlier the Hogatza-Todadonten band may have represented two distinct bands, one east of the Koyukuk around Lake Todadonton and the other to the west in the Hogatza drainage. Sometime around 1867 these people were decimated by disease and the remaining families joined one another near the Koyukuk."[4] Alexander, the Gwich'in man who became the South Fork band patriarch and who came from Too Loghe (Talowa on Olsons Lake), married Kaudtena and Ervin from Huslia-Dalbi-Hogatza regional band.[5] All of his descendants became known as the South Fork Band. He returned to Kanuti Lake and Konumunket

---

* Since the ethnonym for themselves has never been elicited I will use these river names as the regional band name for this group.

area about 1860 (he would have been about 15 years old) and then moved up to the Southfork-Henshaw Creek-Lower Alatna region about 1874.[6]

As for the Too Loghe Hut'aane Koyukon regional band on Chehłee Van (Chandalar Lake), they remained in that area until the 1850s when, much to the alarm of the locals, they first started coming down into the Yukon Flats. It appears that they made a foiled attempt to retaliate in the fall of 1850 against the Taghe Chox Xut'ana Lower Tanana after their March 1850 raid on Sełyee Menkk'et on the upper Kk'oonootne (Kanuti River). The Too Loghe Hut'aane Koyukon, named the K'iitł'it Gwich'in by the Gwich'in, remained in the upper Koyukuk River until at least 1892. The John Star family of Tanana and the mother of Uloudin from Galena came from the Too Loghe Hut'aane Koyukon.[7] By this time, many of them had moved eastward, intermarrying with the decimated Gwich'in populations. A few families settled at Hudochaaget and since the Allakaket connection is so strong, at least a few must have married into that community.

By 1851, the Di'haii Gwich'in were just barely hanging on in the upper Koyukuk River and, after the death of Dits'ii K'iitł'uu in 1855, his whole extended family moved onto Neets'aii, Draanjik, Vantee, Dagoo and Teetł'it Gwichin,* and Taghe Chox Xut'ana Lower Tanana estates. John Vindeegwizhii, Tr'ootsyaa, Robert Shoh Vat T'oo, and Shanavee were already moved onto the Neets'aii and Draanjik estates between 1864 and 1866. Vats'ach'arahthan (and probably others) moved to Peel River and onto the Teetł'it estate among the Eastern Gwich'in. No one seems to know what happened to Dits'ii K'iitł'uu's son, Gook'aahtii, who was living along the Lower Ramparts. The last time he appears in the Hudson's Bay journals is on June 14, 1851, but he is on the Debtors Sheet in 1855. Unless he had another name (which my father did not know), there is no record of him in McDonald's journals which began on the Yukon Flats in 1862. As late as 1866, McDonald mentions two Indians from the

---

* Eastern Gwich'in nation along the Peel River.

camp of the Siffluer Indians (Di'hạịị Gwich'in) visiting at Fort Yukon. So there may have been a few stragglers that remained in the area, as Kennicott said there were four hunters left among them in 1861. If we recall, F. C. Schrader ran into Mary Ch'iyikgwadhah's family near Horace Mountain in June of 1899. Mary's son, Robert, was educated at the mission school at Ramparts on the Yukon.[8] John C. Cantwell stated, "On December 6, all the Indians living at Rampart House, a native settlement situated on the Yukon 6 miles above Dall River, came down to pay a visit on their kinsmen at our place."[9] This must have been the Rampart House where Robert was educated. That survivors of the Lower Ramparts Di'hạịị Gwich'in community moved onto the Neets'ạịị estate can be established, since they are the ones who recounted the murder of five of their number in the Lower Ramparts to Mercier. All the Di'hạịị Gwich'in except for Alexander of Too Loghe were dispersed to the east. The Di'hạịị Gwich'in abandoned their estate in the mid 1850s, but as Neets'ạịị Gwich'in they continued to live in the upper Koyukuk until at least 1867 and the early 1870s.

The Taghe Chox Xut'ana Lower Tanana were traveling with the Menhtee Xut'ana in 1864.[10] The Taghe Chox Xut'ana hung on until the scarlet fever epidemic of 1865–66, when they were almost completely wiped out. Out of twenty men in 1847, eight men died in 1866 and four men had died in 1864. McDonald noted in June of 1866 that only three men, two boys, three women, and six children remained.[11] At the time they were camped near the vicinity of King Slough. McDonald's interpreter at the sight was Bayitinukwulta, a man who visited Fort Yukon the previous winter. Two women were absorbed into the Gwichyaa and/or Draanjik estates.[12] One of them, Maria, was married to Old Henry Peter and was also the maternal grandmother of the late Sophie Paul of Fort Yukon, Alaska.[13] Dall and Whymper ascended the river in 1867 and after passing the Dall River, Dall said, "Passed by several deserted houses formerly inhabited by some Indians of the Kutchin tribes, who all died five years ago of the scarlet fever...From the Chilkáht Indians it spread to those of the Upper Yukon, and down the river to this point, where all died and the disease spent itself. These are known to the English as the Small Houses, and the locality is an excellent one for game and fish of all kinds."[14] Dall may have been told that they were of the "Kutchin tribes" by his two "Nucklúkahyét' Indian guides who were probably Yookkene or Noghee Hut'aane Koyukon people of the Yukon River below the confluence of the Tozitna River. On the same trip Whymper said, "On the river below Fort Yukon, a people almost extinct the "Gens de Mileau" once lived; but the ravages—in this case, of scarlet fever—have hardly left one to tell the tale."[15] This tells us that in the spring of 1867 no Taghe Chox Xut'ana were living in the area of the Dall River. Charles W. Raymond on his 1869 trip down the Yukon River wrote after leaving Fort Yukon, "The first native village met with in descending the river is situated on the right hand bank, just below the Rampart Rapids."[16] This was the summer fish camp of Shahnyaati'. The Taghe Chox Xut'ana Lower Tanana were completely disbanded as of 1866.

When was the area of the Taghe Chox Xut'ana estate repopulated? We know from Raymond's report that there was no village in 1869. One-and-a-half day's journey above the confluence of the Tanana and Yukon rivers McDonald ran into a camp of "Tetsi Kutchin" that consisted of twelve men, eleven women and seventeen children which could be in the vicinity of Fort Hamlin. Leonard John, "The three brothers [Jacob (b. circa 1840[17] d. 1914[18]), Gochonayeeya and Old Steven(b. circa 1837)[19]] that went down to Kokrines moved back up here with their families and two or three other families came with them too...So when their brother, Charlie [b. circa 1850[20]],* over on the Koyukuk [River] heard that his brothers had moved back here, he moved over and brought some families...At

---

* Leonard John says that Charlie was older than Old Steven and that Jacob was the oldest brother. You can see how the census takers were guessing at their ages. Their order of birth was: Jacob, Gochonayeeya, Charlie, and Old Steven. Gochonayeeya was their first chief.

the time this place here was called Denyeet [from Gwich'in *danzhit*[21]] which means canyon in the Athabascan Indian language."[22] People started moving back into the area in 1870. In 1873, a trapper by the name of Leroy McQuesten came down the river and found a community in the Ramparts.[23] According to John Taylor White who was at the mouth of Dall River in 1898, "The natives now living together at the mouth of Dall River once lived in widely separated districts. Most of them have come from a village called Hor-tar-chaket* on the Koyukuk River near the mouth of Old Man Creek [Kk'oonootne]. Some have come from Fort Yukon at the mouth of the Porcupine River. One family from the mouth of the Tanana River, one from Chandaleur River, and one from Noritna River [Nowitna]. The remaining families belong to this part of the Yukon. A few years ago these latter families were scattered along the right bank of the Yukon on the Dall River near it's mouth."[24] There was a mixed Gwich'in/Lower Tanana/Koyukon community at the mouth of the Dall River called Hudochaaget,[25] but that community had only been in existence for about five years at the time.[26] The Dall River was known as the Tchtaugquanah which means "come down from Tchtau" (Ch'itaa Gwanah).

White continues, "One of the natives here told about Tchets-sul [Ch'itsil], or Old White Eye,...and described him as a "big chief, plenty big fight." Tchets-sul lived at Kesh-tol-ton-ta [the present sight of White Eye on the Yukon] near the mouth of the Chandaleur River,...At one time he ruled all the Indians from Circle to Dall River;...Along time ago the Tananas came over by the Birch Creek and a 'big fight' took place,...Tchets-sul died some three or four years ago,† and since then no one has assumed the name of chief. The present villages are simply communities made up of the surviving remnants of the various tribes,..."[27] K'eesh Doltonh Denh is variously described as being at the mouth of the Lower Birch

---

* Not re-elicited. Maybe the Kornuchaket of Hudson Stuck, 1988: 179.
† On the 4th of July.

Creek,[28] on the north side of the Yukon below Teedriinjik (Chandalar River), and across from the Lower Birch Creek mouth. I would be inclined to believe that it was the latter site. McDonald first speaks of Jitzil[29] and then Chitzil, "Chitzil, alias Archibald Garret* and William Scott arrived this evening from the fish-barriere at Birch River..."[30] McQuesten was near the vicinity of Beaver Creek among some lakes when he mentioned White Eye, "There was an old Indian called White Eye that came down the River about sixty miles. He supplied our dogs and ourselves with meat until we got to Fort Yukon..."[31] Ch'indee K'aa, White Eye† as he was also known, lived in the same locality for a considerable length of time.

The Reverend V. C. Sim of the Church Missionary Society wrote in June 1884, "We here found a man with two women and a child, the sole survivors of a small band of Indians who were carried off by the sickness in the summer of '82."[32] This epidemic might have been diphtheria.[33] In 1883 Schwatka found Senati Village, near the rapids occupied by, "2 well worn tents and 4 birch bark houses there containing forty or fifty souls."[34] By this time Shahnyaati' no longer came to the Lower Ramparts to go fishing.

In 1892 Bishop Bompas wrote to Jules L. Prevost stationed at St. James Mission from Stevens Village, "I find here a band of Indians under a chief named Stephen who are mixed of Tukuth and Totsikutchin Indians and speak partly both languages. The adults nearly all understand the Tukuth...Some are only visiting from camps higher up the River. We are almost half way to old Fort Yukon from your mission...[But I hear of a band of Kitlikutchin across the mountains to the north who have never been taught or baptized at all except 3 men baptized long since by Archdeacon McDonald. That band joins these Indians I learn on the first snow here at the

---

* McDonald baptized the Western Gwich'in with a given name and then just added a last name usually after people who were in the area or had been in the area, like William Lucas Hardisty. Shahnyaati's Christian name was John Hardisty.

† For he literally had one white eye.

River and stay till New Year (They speak the Totsikutchin language)…(The winter distance is about five days from your mission)."[35] This is one of the most direct connections between the Chehłee Van (Chandalar Lake) Too Loghe Hʉt'aane Koyukon and the Yukon River residents of the Stevens Village region.

Aftermath, Chapter Notes

1. Alexander Hunter Murray, *Journal of the Yukon 1847–48*, (Ottowa: Government Printing Bureau, 1910): 11. Raboff, 1999: 14, 15.

2. Nicholas J. Gubser, *"Comparative Study of the Intellectual Culture of the Nunamiut Eskimos at Anaktuvuk Pass, Alaska,"* (Fairbanks: University of Alaska, 1961): 92.

3. Upper Yukon River Koyukon Athapaskan Social Culture: An Overview, proceedings, Northern Athapaskan Conference, 1971, vol. 1, ed. A. McFadyen Clark, Ottawa, 1975.

4. Annette McFayden-Clark, *Koyukuk River Culture*, National Museum of Man Mercury Series, Canadian Ethnology Service Paper No. 18 (1974): 5.

5.McFadyen Clark, *Who Lived in This House? A Study of Koyukuk river Semisubterranean Houses*, Mercury Series, Archaelogical Survey of Canada, Paper 153. (Quebec: Canadian Museum of Civilization, 1996): 66.

6. Donald W. Clark, personal communication, January 1998.

7. Catherine Attla, personal communication, April 1997 and November 1998.

8. F. C. Schrader, diary, United States Geological Survey, Anchorage, Alaska, 1899: 49.

9. John C. Cantwell, *Report of the Operation of the U. S. Revenue Steamer Nunivak on the Yukon River Station, Alaska, 1899–1901* (Washington: Government Printing Office, 1904): 83.

10. McDonald, journal entry, 24 June 1864 (1910).

11. McDonald, journal entry, 2 June 1866 (1910).

12. Ibid.

13. William Schneider, *Beaver, Alaska: The Story of a Multi-Ethnic Community*, paper submitted to the faculty of Bryn Mawr College, 1976: 323.

14. William H. Dall, *Alaska and Its Resources*, 2nd ed. (Arno & The New York Times, 1970): 100.

15. Frederick Whymper, *Transactions of the Ethnological Society of London, Vol. VII, New Series* (London: Ethnological Society of London and John Murray, Albemarle Street, London, 1869): 178.

16. Captain Charles W. Raymond, Report of a Resonnassance of the Yukon River, Alaska Territory, July to September 1869, Washington Government Press Office, 1871.

Raymond, 1981: 22.

17. 1900 Census.

18. Leonard John, "How Stevens Village Came To Be," *Alaska Sportsman*, (September 1959): 32.

19. Ibid.

20. Ibid.

21. Margaret Matthews, et.al., "Stevens Village Land Use Plan, Ethnogeography of Ancestral Lands and Integrated Resources Management Plan," (Stevens Village, Alaska: Stevens Village Council, 1999): 86.

22. John, 1959.

23. Leroy N. McQuesten, "Recollections of Leroy N. McQuesten," *Life in the Yukon, 1871–1885* (Dawson City, Canada: Yukon Order of Pioneers, June 1852): 3.

24. James Taylor White, University of Alaska Archives, Box III, fo. 27: 1.

25. Matthews, et. al., 1999: 54

26. John Taylor White, A partial list of words and phrases used by the Ten'a Indians living in the vicinity of Fort Shoemaker, Dall River, Alaska, ms., University of Alaska Archives.

27. White, Box III, fo. 27, p. 7.

28. Matthews, et. al., 1999:82.

29. McDonald, journal entry, 6 October 1868.

30. Ibid., journal entry, 16 November 1868.

31. McQuesten, 1952: 3.

32. V. C. Sim, letter to Church Missionary Society from Rampart House, 9 January 1885, The Anglican Church of Canada, General Synod Archives, Toronto, Ontario, Canada; LPCMS(L), Reel A-113, Group MG17B2,

33. Robert Fortuine, *Chills and Fever, Health and Disease in the Early History of Alaska* (Fairbanks: University of Alaska Press, 1992): 214.

34. Schwatka, 1883: 299.

35. Jules L. Prevost, letter from J. L. Prevost to Rev. Doctor Langford, 7 September 1892, Episcopal Church Archives, Domestic and Foreign Missionary Society, Austin, Texas, Alaska Papers 1889–1939.

CONCLUSION

In this book I have introduced the Nendaaghe Hʉt'aane Koyukon of the Howard Pass area, upper Noatak, Itivliim Kuuŋa (Etivluk), and Aalaasuuraq (Nigu) rivers and delineated the estates of the Saakił Hʉt'aane Koyukon of the upper Kobuk River, the Too Loghe Hʉt'aane Koyukon and Di'hąįį Gwich'in of the upper Koyukuk River, and have identified and established the Taghe Chox Xut'ana Lower Tanana along the Yukon River between Dall River and the Lower Birch Creek mouth. Their history began in obscurity: language, cultural bias, and inaccessibility hid their histories for over a hundred and fifty years.

The Northern Koyukon and the Nendaaghe and Too Loghe Hʉt'aane Koyukon, have been particularly mysterious—like the *iñuksuich* (plural of *iñuksuk*) that are spread out across the horizon in the Brooks Range, they left only the faintest traces. It was the murmuring about the Iyaġaaġmiut and Uyaġaaġmiut that persisted into the twentieth century that caught the attention of people like Giddings, Ingstad, Gubser, Hall, Alexander, Anderson, Campbell, Binford, Libby, Spearman, Burch, and Mishler and it made them look for an Athabascan group to which to apply the name. Panniaq, who has been described as the "oral historian extraordinare," gave everyone a direction; "the Chandalar people," "the Fort Yukon people." But in the turmoil of the early to mid ninteenth century, it would have been very difficult for one person to have been exactly in the right place at the right time to piece together every thread of evidence which tied the Northern Koyukon to the Iyaġaaġmiut and Uyaġaaġmiut. Panniaq was indeed a faithful oral historian. Almost none of this history could be written without his account.

The shock of their displacement by 1844 and the loss of family and estate left many Nendaaghe Hʉt'aane Koyukon depressed and unable to talk about their former lives. Aldzak, the father of Sarah Shaaghan Dik (Old lady of the Source), and her half-sister, Nach'ats'an, became a recluse for the rest of his life on the Di'hąįį estate. He built himself a substantial *konh* (semisubterranean house) on or near Chehłee Van (Chandalar Lake) which his grandchildren and great-grandchildren talked about into the mid-twentieth century. Sarah Shaaghan Dik, for her part, talked from morning to night, recanting her personal journeys (both physical and spiritual). Much that survives about life on the Nendaaghe estate survives through her relentless strength and vision. She died a very old lady on the Neets'ąįį estate at the turn of the century.

The Too Loghe Hʉt'aane Koyukon on the upper Koyukuk lived very much like the Di'hąįį Gwich'in to their east. K'ets'eeggaage', the famous medicine man of the Kodeel Kkaakk'e Hʉt'aane Koyukon at the mouth of the Kateel River, named them both in 1842. They had a shared border along the El tseeyh no' (John) and Koyukuk rivers and they both came down to the mouth of the Koyukuk River to trade. They often returned by going up the Yukon River and overland back to the Koyukuk River. It seems that the Too Loghe Hʉt'aane Koyukon had always been intermarried with the Di'hąįį Gwich'in, but after their complete displacement from the northern part of their estate in 1845 and 1846, many of the surviving women became the wives of Dits'ii K'iitł'uu at K'iitł'uu at the mouth of El tseeyh no' (John River). Their displacement was not as severe a shock because they already knew the lay of the land and they were intermarried with the Di'hąįį Gwich'in. Yet their encroachment onto the Di'hąįį estate was not completely peaceful. After being ousted by the Kuukpiġmiut from the northern part of the Too Loghe estate in 1846, there were two regional bands: one regional band along the

Aalaasuk (Alatna River) and upper Kk'oonootne (Kanuti River), the other centered at Chehłee Van (Chandalar Lake). Dits'ii K'iitł'uu was at odds with the Aalaasuk/Kk'oonootne regional band and raided the village of Dobenhdaatltonh Denh near the mouth of the Aalaasuk (Alatna River) in 1847. Then in March of 1850 they were attacked from the south by the Taghe Chox Xut'ana Lower Tanana and Deenduu Gwich'in at Sełyee Menkk'et along the upper Kk'oonootne (Kanuti River). These two battles left almost no survivors of the Aalaasuk/Kk'oonootne regional band. The only person we know for sure is Hʉdughyenee, the grandmother of the late Little Beatus of Allakaket. Meanwhile at Chehłee Van (Chandalar Lake), the Too Loghe Hʉt'aane Koyukon stayed on until the 1890s when they, too, moved eastward onto the vacated Taghe Chox Xut'ana Lower Tanana lands and the Neets'ąįį , Draanjik, Vantee, and Teetł'it Gwich'in estates.

The Di'hąįį Gwich'in were the least known of any of the Gwich'in nations. They were known as the Too Tleekk'e Hʉt'aane by their Koyukon nieghbors to the west. Within the first three years of the establishment of Fort Yukon in 1847, the Di'hąįį Gwich'in were already reduced to one large extended family. In 1847 Dits'ii K'iitł'uu attacked Dobenhdaatltonh Denh and in 1851 there was a devastating attack upon the Gwich'in community of Too Loghe on the shores of Olsons Lake at the headwaters of the Kanuti, Dall, and Ray rivers. Only Alexander, the grandfather of the late Robert Williams of Allakaket survived to adulthood. He intermarried with members of the Huslia-Dalbi-Hogatza nation and later moved back up the Koyukuk River, first to Kk'oonootne (Kanuti River) and then to the area around Henshaw Creek. Meanwhile, other Di'hąįį Gwich'in hung on in the upper Koyukuk River, near the Tlaakk'ołneekk'e (North Fork) and Hʉkkughutono' (Middle Fork), until the death of their patriarch, Dits'ii K'iitł'uu in 1855. After 1855 they moved onto the Neets'ąįį , Deenduu, Draanjik, Vantee, and Teetł'it Gwich'in estates, and later the almost abandoned Taghe Chox Xut'ana Lower Tanana estate.

The Taghe Chox Xut'ana Lower Tanana have been bathed in obscurity since 1867 when Dall and Whymper mentioned them last on their trip up the Yukon River. In 1847 they numbered twenty men (a possible total population of 120) and they had been embroiled in two wars within the first three years of the forts establishment in Fort Yukon. The first war was fought in 1847 with the aide of the Di'hąįį Gwich'in against the Menhtee Xut'ana Lower Tanana of the Minto Flats and their Noghee and Yookkene Hʉt'aane Koyukon allies at Tohot'onhde (Morelock Creek). The second battle was an attack on the Too Loghe Hʉt'aane Koyukon at Sełyee Menkk'et along the upper Kk'oonootne (Kanuti River). Some of Shahnyaati's Deenduu Gwich'in joined in that attack. They suffered illness in the winter of 1847–48 and starvation during the winter of 1849–50. In 1866, after the scarlet fever epidemic, they were down to three men, two boys, three women, and six children. Two women were immediately married off upriver. Then they simply disappeared. In 1870, people reappeared in the vicinity of the Lower Ramparts and began a new community, but they did not speak Taghe Chox Xut'ana Lower Tanana; they spoke Koyukon, an upper Koyukuk dialect.

While this history has been about the Northern Koyukon, Western Gwich'in, and Lower Tanana people, it has included the histories, however brief, of the Akuniġmiut Inupiat of the central Kobuk, the Nuataaġmiut of the upper Noatak River, the Tikiġaġmiut of Point Hope, the Kuukpiġmiut (Qaŋmaliġmiut, Killiġmiut, and Kaŋianiġmiut regional bands) of the Kuukpik (Colville River), the Kuuvaum Kaŋiaġmiut of the upper Kobuk River, and the Nunamiut of Anaktuvuk Pass as well as the Saakił, Kodeel Kkaakk'e, Noghee, and Yookkene Hʉt'aane Koyukon nations and the Huslia-Dalbi-Hogatza nation.

From its inception, this book has been a voyage of discovery. I started with the basic idea to do a history of the Gwich'in people going from west to east, but in the process had to include the Northern Koyukon for, as it came to be, they are the ancestors of the present day Gwich'in people of the Yukon Flats. Also, it was my intention to disprove the notion that the Di'haịị Gwich'in themselves originated in the upper Noatak River valley. While disproving this notion, I discovered that the Northern Koyukon were in the Chehłee Van (Chandalar Lake) area in the mid 1840s, much earlier than I had thought.

I always wondered how Simon Paneak and others of Anaktuvuk Pass made the connection between the Uyaġaaġmiut and the "Chandalar people, and the Fort Yukon people," but I had forgotten the winters of the 1910s, 1920s, and 1930s when the Nunamiut would spend them in the vicinity of Old John Lake (Van K'eedii) and the upper Khiinjik (Sheenjik River) valley. What really tied these events to the Fort Yukon people in their minds was a chance meeting with John Vindeegwizhii in the late 1920s when Simon Paneak, Billy Morry, and Elijah Kakinya came to Fort Yukon to trade. Vindeegwizhii verily railed at them in a public place. They were all frightened by that event and the meeting that was called by the chief of Fort Yukon on the following day was even more ominous, not only because of the language barrier, but because they were also outside of their estate. They learned then that Vindeegwizhii had been a child at the time of the Anaktuvuk Pass displacement. But Simon and the others could never have known about the transition from one estate to another and the language changes that had to take place. Yet the Nunamiut kept a faithful oral record of events that happened over a century and a half ago.

Then, beginning in 1847, there were the convoluted, mixed up accounts of Alexander Hunter Murray, William Lucas Hardisty, Strachen Jones, and others of the Hudson's Bay Company in Fort Yukon. They were convuluted and mixed up because the same terms were used to describe different nations. Somehow events came together after I gathered notes by McKennan and Hadleigh-West, snipits of information from Annette McFadyen Clark, McDonalds journal entries, McQuesten's autobiography, Merçier's recollections, an article by the late Leonard John of Stevens Village, and Peter John's (of Minto) interviews that came about in 1999 along with earlier interviews done by Bill Schneider of the Oral History Department at the University of Alaska Fairbanks. It took all of these sources to flesh out the Hudson's Bay Company records and what actually happened in the Lower Ramparts.

Finally, none of these things would have come about if it were not for the oral records of my father, the late Stephen Steven Tsee Gho' Tsyaa Tsal Peter, Sr. Beginning in 1966, I started a family tree project with my great-aunt through marriage, the late Sophie Ch'eelil John, of Venetie, Alaska. At the time I was satisfied with our immediate family, but I had inadvertently triggered memories in Ch'eelil's mind. She talked about family and family histories in every direction for a hundred years before that, and for two weeks straight, but much to our great loss, I could not keep up with her. Some of the connections she established are only vague memories. It is unfortunate that we were not able to record her at the time. When I started working with my father in 1987, I taped a few sessions, but mostly I wrote down notes on little scraps of paper that I threw into a large box. That box got bigger and finally I fed it all into a computer. But even after working with my father for ten years we still had to write, rewrite, and edit our family tree until we made the right connections. Furthermore, other people made connections that my father could not have known about—mainly Mae Peter Wallis, Frank Ginnis, Hester Evan, Mary Nim Ch'u' Thompson, and my mother, Katherine Joseph Peter. When looking into the Episcopal Church records and the census of 1900, 1910, and 1920, I found that my father's recounting of families and family members was extraodinarily accurate. He was in the habit of recounting people in the traditional way, by order of birth. I have dedicated this work, which could not have happened without him, to the memory of my father.

Northern Koyukon, Gwich'in, and Lower Tanana Timeline

1250–1400	Northern Koyukon begin to expand from the upper Kobuk into the upper Noatak River drainage.
1800–1820	Nendaaghe Hʉt'aane Koyukon communities at Atłiq Lake and along the upper Nunataaq (Noatak River) are attacked by Iñupiat. The weather cools. Famine begins in Northwestern Alaska.
1821–1826	The Nendaaghe Hʉt'aane Koyukon retaliate with an attack on Nuvuġaluaq, a suburb of Point Hope, on the Tikiġaq Iñupiat estate. They wipe out that community. The following year they return and are ambushed.
1820–1840	One band of Nendaaghe Hʉt'aane Koyukon flee southward to the upper Kobuk River onto the Saakił estate. The Nendaaghe Hʉt'aane Koyukon and the Nuataaġmiut Iñupiat ambush and raid each other along the upper Kobuk and Noatak rivers.
	The Kuukpiġmiut Iñupiat push southward into the upper Aalaasuuraq (Nigu River). The Nuataaġmiut Iñupiat push up the Noatak River.
1839–1840	The Saakił and Nendaaghe Hʉt'aane Koyukon have an all out battle along the upper Kobuk River. The Saakił Hʉt'aane Koyukon call upon their downriver relatives the Akuniġmiut Iñupiat for assistance. The Nendaaghe Hʉt'aane Koyukon are defeated along the upper Kobuk River and move northward.

1841–1844	The Nendaaghe Hʉt'aane Koyukon are driven from Nendaaghe and join the Too Loghe Hʉt'aane Koyukon to the east.
1845–1847	Nendaaghe and Too Loghe Hʉt'aane Koyukon make their last stand along the Killik River. They are defeated.
1846–1847	The Nendaaghe and Too Loghe Hʉt'aane Koyukon are defeated by the Kuukpiġmiut Iñupiat at K'iitł'it/ Anaktuvuk Pass. They attempt to regroup, but are found starving and malnourished along the Killik River in the following year.
1846–1848	The remainder of the Nendaaghe and Too Loghe Hʉt'aane Koyukon retreat to two communities, Dobenhdaatltonh Denh near the mouth of Aalaasuk (Alatna River) and Sełyee Menkk'et along the upper Kanuti River within the Too Loghe estate. They encroah upon the Di'haii estate at Chehłee Van (Chandalar Lake). They intermarry with the Neets'aii Gwich'in.
1847	Dits'ii K'iitł'uu khaihkwaii attacks Dobenhdaatltonh Denh north of Allakaket, Alaska. He takes four women and children captive. John Ch'ijinjaa and his mother Neeshih are among them. Neshih becomes one of his wives, Ch'ijinjaa is driven away and joins his relative, Làrryil north of Van K'eedii (Old John Lake), and becomes a lifelong Neets'aii Gwich'in.
	Battle at Tohot'onhde (Morelock Creek): Menhtee Xut'ana Lower Tanana joined by Noghee and Yookk'ene Hʉt'aane Koyukon verses Di'haii Gwich'in, Too Loghe Hʉt'aane, and Taghe Chox Lower Tanana. Shahnyaati' is foiled in his attempt to attack the Di'haii Gwich'in.
1848	Menhtee and Taghe Chox Lower Tanana continue ambush and raiding.
1849–1850	Areawide famine and illness surrounding Fort Yukon.

March 1850	Taghe Chox Xut'ana Lower Tanana and Deenduu Gwich'in wipe out the Too Loghe Hʉt'aane Koyukon community of Sełyee Menkk'et along the Kk'oonootne (Kanuti River).
July 1850	Too Loghe Hʉt'aane Koyukon come down onto the Yukon Flats with Shahnyaati' as their escort.
March 1851	Menhtee Xut'ana Lower Tanana and Deenduu Gwich'in wipe out Di'haii Gwich'in community of Too Loghe on Olsons Lake. Alexander the grandfather of Robert Williams of Allakaket, Alaska survives. His brothers, sister, and mother are taken captive along the Yukon River. His mother dies at Hʉdochaaget at the mouth of Dall River.
1855	The Di'haii Gwich'in move eastward after the death of Dits'ii K'iitł'uu onto the Neets'aii, Gwichyaa, Deenduu, Draanjik, Vantee, and Teetł'it estates.
1855–1867	Too Loghe Hʉt'aane Koyukon (also known as K'iitł'it Gwich'in by the Gwich'in people) at Chehłee Van (Chandalar Lake) begin their eastward movement into the Yukon Flats.
1870	The former Taghe Chox estate is repopulated by Koyukon, Gwich'in, and Lower Tanana.
1898	Ch'itsil the chief of the Denyee Hʉt'aane dies.

Bibliography

Alexander, Herbert. "Prehistory of the Central Brooks Range—An Archaeological Analysis." Ph.D. diss., University of Oregon. Ann Arbor, Mich.: University Microfilms, 1969.

————. Putu: A Fluted Point Site In Alaska, Simon Fraser University, Department of Archaeology, Publication No. 17, Burnaby, B. C., Canada, 1987.

Allen, Henry T. An Expedition to The Copper, Tanana and Koyukuk Rivers 1885. Anchorage, Alaska: Northwest Publishing Co., 1985.

Anderson, Douglas D. "An Archaeological Survey of Noatak Drainage, Alaska," Arctic Anthropology 9, no. 1 (1972): 66–102.

Anderson, Douglas, and Wanni W. Anderson, Ray Bane, Richard K. Nelson, Nita Sheldon Towarak. Kuuvaŋmiut Subsistence: Traditional Eskimo Life in the Latter Twentieth Century, 1st ed., National Parks Service, 1986; 2d ed., Barrow, Alaska: Northwest Arctic Borough School District, 1992.

Arndt, Katherine Louise. "Dynamics of the Fur Trade on the Middle Yukon, Alaska, 1839–1868," Ph. D. diss., University of Alaska, 1996.

Beechey, Frederick William. Narrative of a Voyage to the Pacific and Beering's Strait, To Cooperate With The Polar Expedition, in the years 1825, 26, 27, 28., 1st ed., London, 1831; 2d ed., New York: Henry Colburn and Richard Bertley, 1968.

Bekk'oyoodaałdleede, Henry. Chief Henry Yugh Nollonigee: The Stories of Chief Henry. Translated and transcribed by Eliza Jones. Fairbanks: Alaska Native Language Center, University of Alaska Fairbanks, 1979.

Bockstoce, J. R. Eskimos of Northwest Alaska In The Early Nineteenth Century, University of Oxford, Pitt Rivers Museum, Monograph Series No. 1. Oxford: Oxprint Limited, 1977.

Burch, Jr., Ernest S. The Traditional Eskimo Hunters of Point Hope, Alaska: 1800–1875. North Slope Borough, 1981.

————. "Boundaries and Borders in Early Contact North-Central Alaska," Arctic Anthropology 35, no. 2 (1998).

————. The Cultural and Natural Heritage of Northwest Alaska, Vol. VII. Kotzebue, Alaska: International Affairs, NANA Museum of the Arctic; Anchorage, Alaska: U. S. National Parks Service, Alaska Region, 1998.

————. The Iñupiaq Eskimo Nations of Northwest Alaska. Fairbanks, Alaska: University of Alaska Press, 1998.

Burch, Jr., Ernest S. and Craig W. Mishler. "The Di'haįį Gwich'in: Mystery People of Northern Alaska," Arctic Anthropology 32, no. 1 (1995): 147–172.

Burch, Jr., Ernest S., and Eliza Jones, Hannah P. Loon, Lawrence D. Kaplan. "The Ethnogenesis of the Kuuvaum Kaŋiaġmiut," Ethnohistory, vol. 46, no. 2 (1999).

Campbell, John M. "Cultural Session at Anaktuvuk Pass, Arctic Alaska," pp. 39–54 in Prehistoric Cultural Relations Between the Arctic and Temperate Zones of North America. Edited by John Campbell. Arctic Institute of North America, Technical Paper No. 11, 1969.

————. "The Kavik Site of Anaktuvuk Pass, Central Brooks Range, Alaska," Anthropological papers of the University of Alaska 14, no. 1 (1968): 32–42.

Cantwell, John C. "A Narrative of the Exploration of the Kowak River, Alaska," Report of the Cruise of the Revenue Marine Steamer Corwin in the Arctic Ocean, U. S. Revenue Cutter Service, Washington, D. C., 1885.

Caulfield, Richard A. and Walter Peter. Subsistence Division, Alaska Department of Fish and Game, Maps U. S. Geological Survey 250,000 Series, 1982.

Clark, Donald W. and A. McFadyen Clark. Batza Ten'a, Trail of Obsidian, Archaeology at an Alaskan Obsidian Source, Archaeological Survey of Canada Mercury Series Paper 147, Canadian Museum of Civilization, 1993.

Dall, W. H. Alaska and Its Resources, 1st ed., Boston, 1870; 2d ed., Arno & The New York Times, 1970. (Map Showing Distribution of the Native Tribes of Alaska and Adjoining Territory. Compiled from the latest Authorities by W. H. Dall). Published by N. Peters, Washington, #G4371/E1/1875/D37, Falk, University of Alaska Archives.

de Laguna, Frederica. The Prehistory of Northern North America as Seen From the Yukon, The Society For American Archaeology, no. 3, Of Memoirs of the Society, Menasha, Wisconsin, 1947.

Etalook, Arctic John. Recorded oral history. Interviewed and transcribed by Louise M. Riley. Barrow, Alaska: North Slope Borough, #00649trl, tape #60, and 00637trl, tape 31–32, November, 1982. Audiocassette.

Frank, Johnny and Sarah. Neerihiinjik: We Traveled From Place To Place. Edited by Craig Mishler. Fairbanks, Alaska: Alaska Native Language Center, University of Alaska, 1995.

Gerlach, S. Craig and Edwin S. Hall, Jr. "The Later Prehistory of Northern Alaska: The View from Tukuto Lake," Alaska Anthropological Association Monograph Series #4. Fairbanks, Alaska: University of Alaska Fairbanks, 1988.

Giddings, Jr., J. L. "Dendrochronology in Northern Alaska," University of Alaska Publication, vol. 4, 1942.

————. "The Denbigh Flint Complex," American Antiquity 16, no. 3 (1951): 193–202.

————. "Kobuk River People", Studies of Northern Peoples, no. 1. Fairbanks, Alaska: Department of Anthropology and Geography, University of Alaska, 1961.

————. "Alaska Aboriginal Culture," National Survey of Historic Sites and Buildings, theme XVI. Anchorage, Alaska: Indigenous Peoples and Cultures, National Parks Service, Anchorage Area Office, 1962.

Gubser, Nicholas J. "Comparative Study of Intellectual Culture of the Nunamiut Eskimos of Anaktuvuk Pass, Alaska," Manuscript, University of Alaska, 1961.

_____. The Nunamiut: Hunters of Caribou. Yale University Press, 1965.

Hadleigh-West, Frederick. "On the Distribution and Territories of Western Kutchin Tribes," Anthropological Papers of the University of Alaska 7, no. 2, (1959).

_____. The Netsi Kutchin: An Essay in Human Ecology. Ph. D. diss., in Anthropology, submitted to Louisiana State University and Agricultural and Mechanical College, Baton Rouge, Louisiana, 1963.

Hall, Jr., Edwin S. "Speculation on the Late Prehistory of the Kutchin Athapaskans," Ethnohistory 16, no. 4, (1969).

_____. "The Late Prehistoric/Early Historic Eskimos of Interior Northern Alaska: An Ethnoarcheological Approach?" Anthropological Papers of the University of Alaska 15, no. 1, (1970).

_____. "Kutchin Athapaskan/Nunamiut Eskimo Conflict," The Alaska Journal 5, no. 4, (1975).

_____. "An Archaeological Survey of Interior Northwest Alaska," Anthropological Papers of the University of Alaska 17, no. 2, (1975).

_____. "A Preliminary Analysis of House Types at Tukuto Lake, Northern Alaska," The Interior Peoples of Northern Alaska, Edited by Edwin S. Hall, Jr., Archaeological Survey of Canada Paper No. 49, National Museum of Man, Ottawa, 1976.

Helms, June, ed., Handbook of North American Indians, Vol. 6, Subarctic. Washington D. C.: Smithsonian Institute Press, 1981: 771

Henzie, Moses. Moses Henzie. Yukon-Koyukuk School District. Vancouver, B. C.: Hancock House Publishers Ltd., 1979.

Herbert, Belle. Shandaa: In My Lifetime. Edited by Bill Pfisterer and Jane McGary. Fairbanks, Alaska: Alaska Native Language Center, 1988.

Hopson, Flossie. North Slope Elders Conference, Barrow, Alaska, May 1978.

Huntington, Sydney and Jim Reardon. Shadows on the Koyukuk. Portland: Alaska Northwest Books, 1998.

Ingstad, Helge. Nunamiut, W. W. Norton & Co., 1954.

Irving, William N. Preliminary Report of an Archaeological Reconnaissance in the Western part of the Brooks Range of Alaska. Cambridge, Ma: Peabody Museum, Harvard University, 1954.

Jette, Jules. Jules Jette. Fairbanks, Alaska: Alaska Native Language Center, University of Alaska Fairbanks.

_____. Jules Jette. On the Geographical names of the Ten'a. Ms. file 14, drawer 13. Spokane: Gonzaga University, 1910.

_____. Koyukon Athabascan Dictionary, ms. Fairbanks, Alaska: Alaska Native Language Center, University of Alaska, 1999.

John, Leonard. "How Stevens Village Came To Be," Alaska Sportsman, September (1959).

Jones, Eliza and Jules Jette. Koyukon Athabascan Dictionary, ms. Fairbanks, Alaska: Alaska Native Language Center, University of Alaska, 1999.

Jones, Strachan. "The Kutchin Tribes." Notes on the Tenneh or Chepewyan Indians of British and Russian America. Annual Report. Smithsonian Institute, 1866.

Kennicott, Robert. Manuscript No. 203-b. Washington D.C.: U. S. National Anthropological Archives, Smithsonian Institution, 1862.

Krauss, Michael E. Native Peoples and Languages of Alaska, Revised Edition. Map. Fairbanks, Alaska: Alaska Native Language Center, University of Alaska Fairbanks, 1982.

Krech, III, Shepard. "On The Aboriginal Population Of The Kutchin," Arctic Anthropology 15-1. (1978).

Lee, Linda Piquk and Ruthie Tatqaviñ Sampson, Edward Tennant. Lore of the Iñupiat. Vol. 3. Northwest Arctic Borough School District, 1992.

Loyens, William J. The Changing Culture of the Nulato Koyukon Indians. Ph. D. diss., University of Wisconsin, Madison. Ann Arbor, Mi.: University of Microfilms, 1975.

McClellan, Catherine. "History of Research in the Subarctic Cordellera." In Handbook of North American Indians, Vol. 6. Washington D. C.: Smithsonian Institution, 1981.

McDonald, Robert. Journal of Robert McDonald. Fairbanks, Alaska: Alaska Native Language Center, University of Alaska, 1910.

McFadyen-Clark, Annette. "Upper Koyukuk River Koyukon Athapaskan Social Culture: an Overview." Proceedings: Northern Athapaskan Conference, 1971. Vol. 1. Edited by A. McFadyen Clark. Ottawa, 1975.

_____. Koyukuk River Culture, Canadian Ethnology Service Paper No. 18. Ottawa: National Museums of Canada, 1974.

_____. "Koyukon," Handbook of North American Indians, Subarctic. Vol. 6. Edited by June Helms. (1981): 582–601.

_____. Who lived in this House? A Study of Koyukuk River Semisubterranean Houses. Mercury Series, Archaeological Survey of Canada, paper no. 153. Quebec: Canadian Museum of Civilization, 1998.

McKennan, Robert A. The Chandalar Kutchin. Arctic Institute of North America Technical Paper No. 17. Montreal, 1965.

_____. "Anent the Kutchin Tribes," American Anthropologist 37, no. 2, (1935).

Maguire, Rochfort. The Journal of Rochfort Maguire. Edited by John Bockstoce. London: The Hakluyt Society, 1988.

Matthews, Margaret, Dave Lacy, James Kari, Randy Mayo. "Stevens Village Land Use Plan, Ethnogeography of Ancestral Lands, And Integrated Resource Management Plan." Stevens Village, Alaska: Stevens Village Council, 1999.

Mendenhall, Hannah, and Ruthie Sampson, Edward Tennant. Lore of the Iñupiat. Vol. 1. Kotzebue, Alaska: Northwest Arctic Borough School District, 1992.

Mendenhall, Walter C. Reconnaisance from Fort Hamlin to Kotzebue Sound, Alaska by way of Dall, Kanuti, Allen, Kowak Rivers. 1902.

Mercier, François Xavier. Recollections of the Youkon: Memoires from the Years 1868–1885. Edited by Linda Fin Yarborough. Anchorage, Alaska: The Alaska Historical Society, 1986.

Morlan, Richard E. The Later Prehistory of the Middle Porcupine Drainage, Northern Yukon Territory. Mercury Series, Archaeological Survey of Canada, Paper No. 11. Ottawa: National Museums of Canada, 1973.

Murdoch, John. "Ethnological Results of the Point Barrow Expedition." 9th Annual Report of the Bureau of American Ethnology for Years 1887–1888. Washington, D. C., (1892): 19–441.

Murray, Alexander Hunter. Journal of the Yukon, 1847–48, Ottawa: Government Printing Bureau, 1910.

Osgood, Cornelius. Contributions to the Ethnography of the Kutchin. Yale University Publications in Anthropology, no. 14, 1936.

Paneak, Simon. American Indian Oral History Collection. Transcript of interview. University of New Mexico, Center for Southwest Research, Collection #MSS 314 BC, Box 22, Folder 8, Tape #842, 1971.

Raboff, Adeline Peter. "Preliminary Study of the Western Gwich'in Bands." American Indian Culture and Research Journal 23, no. 2, (1999): 1–25.

Raymond, Captain Charles W. Report of a Resonnaissance of the Yukon River, Alaska Territory, July to September, 1869. Washington: Government Press Office, 1871.

Ruggles, Richard I. A Country So Interesting. Plate 57. McGill-Queen's University Press, Montreal & Kingston, 1991.

Schneider, William. Beaver, Alaska: The Story of a Multi-Ethnic Community, Paper submitted to the faculty of Bryn Mawr College, 1976.

Schoenberg, Kenneth M. "The Archaeology of Kurupa Lake." Anchorage, Alaska: United States Department of the Interior, National Parks Service, 1985.

Schrader, Frank Charles. Across the Rocky Mountains, along Koyukuk, John, Anaktuvuk, and Colville Rivers and the Arctic Coast to Cape Lisbourne. In 1901.

Sherwood, Morgan B. Exploration of Alaska 1865–1900. Fairbanks, Alaska: University of Alaska Press, 1992.

Skoog, Ronald O. "Ecology of the Caribou in Alaska." Ph.D. diss., University of California, Berkley, 1968.

Stoney, George M. Exploration of Alaska. In U. S. Naval Institute Proceedings of September and December 1899; 2d ed., Seattle: The Shorey Book Store, 1900.

Sun, Joe. My Life and Other Stories. Translated by Susie Sun, edited by David Libbey. NANA Museum of the Arctic with Alaska Humanities Forum, March 1985.

Van Stone, James and Ives Goddard. "Territorial Groups of West-Central Alaska Before 1898." Handbook of North American Indians. Vol. 6. Edited by June Helms. Washington D. C.: Smithsonian Institute, 1981.

Warbelow, Cindie and David Roseneau, Peter Stern. "The Kutchin Caribou Fences of Northeastern Alaska And The Northern Yukon," Biological Report Series. Vol. 32. In Studies of Large Mammals Along the Proposed Mackenzie Valley Gal Pipeline Route From Alaska to British Columbia.   Edited by R. D. Jakimchuk, October, 1975.

Williams, Henry Taa'val. Kọ̀'ehdan. Transcribed by Moses P. Gabriel. Fairbanks, Alaska: Alaska Native Language Center, n.d.

White, John Taylor. Synopsis of Dall River Indians. University of Alaska Archives, 1898–1900.

_____. University of Alaska Archives. Box 4. Undated notebook. March 21.

_____. A Partial list of words and phrases used by the Ten'a Indians living in the vicinity of Fort Shoemaker, Dall River, Alaska. Ms. University of Alaska Archives.

Whymper, Frederick. Travel and Adventure in the Territory of Alaska, 1st ed., London, 1868; 2d ed., Readex Microprint Corporation, 1966.

_____. Transactions of the Ethnological Society of London. Vol. 7, New Series. London: Ethnological Society of London; John Murray, Albemarle Street, London, 1869: 178.

Wright, Miranda. "The Last Great Indian War (Nulato 1851)." Unpublished master's thesis. Fairbanks, Alaska: Department of Anthropology, 1995.

Zagoskin, L. A. Lieutenant Zagoskin's Travels In Russian America 1842–1844: The First Ethnographic and Geographic Investigations in the Yukon and Kuskokwim Valley of Alaska. Edited by Henry N. Michael. Ontario: University of Toronto Press, 1967.

Additional Sources

Hudson's Bay Company Archives, Winnipeg

The General Synod Archives, Toronto

Index

ABOUT THE AUTHOR

Adeline Peter Raboff is a Neets'ạịị Gwich'in Indian, formerly from Arctic Village, Alaska. Ms. Raboff received her degree in history from the University of Alaska Fairbanks in 1997. She currently resides in Fairbanks, Alaska.